Guide to Criminal Law for Illinois

Deborah Lantermo

Attorney at Law

THOMSON

━━━━★━━━━ ™

WADSWORTH

Australia • Canada • Mexico • Singapore • Spain • United Kingdom • United States

Printed in the United States of America
2 3 4 5 6 7   08 07 06 05

Printer: West Group

For more information about our products, contact us at:
Thomson Learning Academic Resource Center
1-800-423-0563

For permission to use material from this text or product, submit a request online at
http://www.thomsonrights.com.
Any additional questions about permissions can be submitted by email to **thomsonrights@thomson.com.**

Library of Congress Control Number: 2004110546

ISBN: 0-534-64416-3

Thomson Wadsworth
10 Davis Drive
Belmont, CA 94002-3098
USA

Asia
Thomson Learning
5 Shenton Way #01-01
UIC Building
Singapore 068808

Australia/New Zealand
Thomson Learning
102 Dodds Street
Southbank, Victoria 3006
Australia

Canada
Nelson
1120 Birchmount Road
Toronto, Ontario M1K 5G4
Canada

Europe/Middle East/South Africa
Thomson Learning
High Holborn House
50/51 Bedford Row
London WC1R 4LR
United Kingdom

Latin America
Thomson Learning
Seneca, 53
Colonia Polanco
11560 Mexico D.F.
Mexico

Spain/Portugal
Paraninfo
Calle/Magallanes, 25
28015 Madrid, Spain

Table of Contents

In Memory of Sam and Trudy
My pals....

CHAPTER ONE

The Origins and Purposes of Criminal Law in Illinois

Each state develops their own criminal laws and sets the penalties for those offenses. Therefore, the definitions of offenses and the terminology used may vary with each state. The Illinois laws addressing the more common offenses of robbery, burglary, and battery for example, are similar to the laws regarding those offenses in many other states. Illinois, however, has created laws covering a wider range of offenses. This book will guide you through some of the nuances of Illinois criminal law.

I. Primary Sources of Criminal Law in Illinois

A. Comments

The primary sources of criminal law in Illinois include:

► State statute
► case law
► U.S. Constitution
► Illinois Constitution
► local ordinance

Criminal laws in Illinois are defined primarily by the state statutes found in the Illinois Criminal Code, more specifically, Chapter 720 of the Illinois Compiled Statutes (ILCS). You will also want to be familiar with Chapter 725 of the ILCS, which governs the procedure in Illinois courts, and Chapter 730 of the ILCS which includes sanctions for criminal offenses. Through case law, the decisions of Illinois judges further define and clarify the law.

The criminal statutes, or laws, must comply with the constitutions of the United States and Illinois. Should a court determine an individual's fundamental rights have been violated, the law will be found unconstitutional. While similar, the Bill of Rights in the Illinois Constitution is not identical to that of the U.S. Constitution. A state constitution may afford greater rights to an individual than our federal constitution.

On the local level, ordinances may be passed to regulate the behavior of individuals within specific counties, cities and villages. An ordinance may proscribe conduct already covered by state statute or may address entirely different behavior.

State statutes evolved from English common law. The Illinois Common Law Act states the common law of England is considered to be in effect until repealed by legislative authority. However, 720 ILCS 5/1-3 states that no conduct constitutes an offense unless it is described as an offense in the Code or in another state statute. In Illinois, the common law crime of rape is now defined as criminal sexual assault.

B. Purposes

The Illinois legislature has stated that the general purposes of the Criminal Code and its provisions are to:
(a) Forbid and prevent the commission of offenses;
(b) Define adequately the act and mental state which constitute each offense, and limit the condemnation of conduct as criminal when it is without fault;
(c) Prescribe penalties which are proportionate to the seriousness of offenses and which permit recognition of differences in rehabilitation possibilities among individual offenders;
(d) Prevent arbitrary or oppressive treatment of persons accused or convicted of offenses.

C. How to Read an Illinois Statute

The statute defining theft is cited as 720 ILCS 5/16-1. As stated above, ILCS refers to the Illinois Compiled Statutes. The number which appears before it refers to the chapter. More specifically, 720 is the chapter on criminal offenses. The number 5 refers to the Act within the chapter. This Act is known as the "Criminal Code of 1961." The number 16 which appears following the slash refers to the Article within the Act. The number 1 refers to the first statute within the Article which happens to define theft. Broken down, it would appear as follows:

Chapter:	720
ILCS:	Illinois Compiled Statutes
Act:	5
Article:	16
Statute:	1

The statute defining theft reads in part:
(a) A person commits theft when he knowingly:
(1) Obtains or exerts unauthorized control over property of the owner; or
(2) Obtains by deception control over property of the owner; or
(3) Obtains by threat control over property of the owner; or
(4) Obtains control over stolen property knowing the property to have been stolen or under such circumstances as would reasonably induce him to believe that the property was stolen;***
(b) Sentence.
(1) Theft of property not from the person and not exceeding $300 in value is a Class A misdemeanor.***
(4) Theft of property from the person not exceeding $300 in value, or theft of property exceeding $300 and not exceeding $10,000 in value, is a Class 3 felony.
(5) Theft of property exceeding $10,000 and not exceeding $100,000 in value is a Class 2 felony.

The statute defining burglary is cited as 720 ILCS 5/19-1. It reads as follows:

(a) A person commits burglary when without authority he knowingly enters or without authority remains within a building, housetrailer, watercraft, aircraft, motor vehicle as defined in The Illinois Vehicle Code [625 ILCS 5/1-100 et seq.], railroad car, or any part thereof, with intent to commit therein a felony or theft. This offense shall not include the offenses set out in Section 4-102 of the Illinois Vehicle Code [625 ILCS 5/4-102].

(b) Sentence. Burglary is a Class 2 felony. A burglary committed in a school or place of worship is a Class 1 felony.

A statute which defines a crime lays out the elements which the prosecutor must establish in order for the defendant to be found guilty. To obtain a conviction for burglary, for example, the State's Attorney would have to establish, among other things, the following elements:

(1) a person
(2) without authority
(3) knowingly
(4) enters, [or] without authority remains
(5) within a building, housetrailer, watercraft, aircraft, motor vehicle, railroad car, [or any part thereof]
(6) with intent to commit therein a felony or theft

D. Ordinances

An example of a city ordinance within Illinois proscribing conduct not otherwise covered by state statute is the City of Wheeling ordinance which reads:

Title 7 ANIMALS
Chapter 7.10 ANIMAL DEPOSITS
7.10.020 Duty to maintain property.

(a) Every person shall maintain the property owned or occupied by that person free from the accumulation of animal deposits. The accumulation of animal deposits means the presence at any one time of more than three distinct deposits of animal excrement.

(b) Where a person who owns or controls an animal occupies a part of a multi-family property such as townhouses, condominiums or apartments, or multi-occupancy commercial or industrial property, that person shall maintain the ground area near that part of the building occupied by that person free of the accumulation of animal deposits. For the purpose of this section, "near" means within thirty feet of any exterior wall of the ground level portion of that part of the building occupied by that person. (Ord. 2686 § A (part), 1991)

E. Web Activity

To view online ordinances for the State of Illinois, visit:

▶URL: http://municode.com/resources/code_list.asp?stateID=13
[Note: an "underscore" appears between "code" and "list" in the above URL.]

II. CLASSIFICATION OF CRIMES

A. Comments

Illinois offenses may be categorized as a petty offense, misdemeanor, or felony. An example of a petty offense would be a speeding ticket. Some offenses may be either a misdemeanor or felony. Theft, for example, may be either a misdemeanor or felony depending upon the conduct involved or the value of the property taken. While some offenses are classified only as misdemeanors, burglary is an example of an offense which is classified only as a felony.

B. Classifications

Offenses are classified in 730 ILCS 5/5-5-1:

> (b) Felonies are classified, for the purpose of sentencing, as follows:
> (1) First degree murder (as a separate class of felony);
> (2) Class X felonies;
> (3) Class 1 felonies;
> (4) Class 2 felonies;
> (5) Class 3 felonies; and
> (6) Class 4 felonies.
>
> (c) Misdemeanors are classified, for the purpose of sentencing, as follows:
> (1) Class A misdemeanors;
> (2) Class B misdemeanors; and
> (3) Class C misdemeanors.

Most statutes state the classification of the offense. However, if none is stated, 720 ILCS 5/5-5-2 provides in part:

> (a) ...Any unclassified offense which is declared by law to be a felony or which provides a sentence to a term of imprisonment for one year or more shall be a Class 4 felony.
> (b) The particular classification of each misdemeanor is specified in the law or ordinance defining the misdemeanor.
> (1) Any offense not so classified which provides a sentence to a term of imprisonment of less than one year but in excess of 6 months shall be a Class A misdemeanor.

(2) Any offense not so classified which provides a sentence to a term of imprisonment of 6 months or less but in excess of 30 days shall be a Class B misdemeanor.

(3) Any offense not so classified which provides a sentence to a term of imprisonment of 30 days or less shall be a Class C misdemeanor.

(c) Any unclassified offense which does not provide for a sentence of imprisonment shall be a petty offense or a business offense.

C. Critical Thinking

►Does a valuation of $300 seem like a good dividing line between misdemeanor and felony theft? Would you change it? Why or why not?

►The legislature did not provide for a misdemeanor level of the offense of burglary. What might have been the reasoning?

►Frankie is 'car hopping' early one morning. He manages to remove the in-dash stereo from one of the vehicles he breaks into and also takes a wallet containing $500 cash. Can the State's Attorney pursue both theft and burglary charges against Frankie? Is the State's Attorney likely to do so? Why or why not?

III. PUNISHMENT

A. Comments

While judges exercise a great deal of discretion when imposing criminal sentences, the maximum period of imprisonment for crimes is set by statute. In addition to fines and the possible imposition of a jail sentence for a misdemeanor conviction or a prison sentence for a felony conviction, judges have other options available to them. For example, offenders who meet certain criteria may qualify to take part in an impact incarceration program. If successfully completed, it may result in a shorter sentence being served.

A defendant sentenced to imprisonment for multiple convictions may be ordered to serve concurrent sentences. Should the judge opine that such a term is required to protect the public from further criminal activity by the defendant, the sentences may run consecutive to one another.

A defendant convicted of murder may still be sentenced to death where deemed appropriate despite the January 31, 2000 moratorium placed on capital punishment in this state. The proposed moratorium continues pending proposed reforms to the system. [See Chapter 9 for more information on the status of the death penalty in Illinois.]

B. Definitions

"Felony" is defined in 730 ILCS 5/5-1-9 as an offense for which a sentence to death or to a term of imprisonment in a penitentiary for one year or more is provided.

"Misdemeanor" is defined in 730 ILCS 5/5-1-14 as any offense for which a sentence to a term of imprisonment in other than a penitentiary for less than one year may be imposed.

"Petty Offense" is defined in 730 ILCS 5/5-1-17 as any offense for which a sentence to a fine only is provided. Petty offenses are not classified.

C. Sanctions

730 ILCS 5/5-8-1 provides in part as follows:
     (a) Except as otherwise provided in the statute defining the offense, a sentence of imprisonment for a felony shall be a determinate sentence set by the court under this Section, according to the following limitations:***

(3) except as otherwise provided in the statute defining the offense, for a Class X felony, the sentence shall be not less than 6 years and not more than 30 years;
(4) for a Class 1 felony, other than second degree murder, the sentence shall be not less than 4 years and not more than 15 years;
(5) for a Class 2 felony, the sentence shall be not less than 3 years and not more than 7 years;
(6) for a Class 3 felony, the sentence shall be not less than 2 years and not more than 5 years;
(7) for a Class 4 felony, the sentence shall be not less than 1 year and not more than 3 years.

730 ILCS 5/5-8-3 provides in part as follows:
     (a) A sentence of imprisonment for a misdemeanor shall be for a determinate term according to the following limitations:
(1) for a Class A misdemeanor, for any term less than one year;
(2) for a Class B misdemeanor, for not more than 6 months;
(3) for a Class C misdemeanor, for not more than 30 days.***

730 ILCS 5/12-7.5 Cyberstalking provides in part as follows:
     (c) Sentence. Cyberstalking is a Class 4 felony. A second or subsequent conviction for cyberstalking is a Class 3 felony.

D. Comments

Enhanced penalties, as evidenced by the theft and burglary statutes, may be imposed based upon the specific conduct of the defendant or, as in the case of cyberstalking, subsequent convictions for the same type of offense.

The Illinois version of "three strikes" provides for a mandatory life sentence for a third or subsequent forcible offense.

720 ILCS 5/33B-1 provides in part as follows:

(a) Every person who has been twice convicted in any state or federal court of an offense that contains the same elements as an offense now classified in Illinois as a Class X felony, criminal sexual assault, aggravated kidnapping or first degree murder, and is thereafter convicted of a Class X felony, criminal sexual assault or first degree murder, committed after the 2 prior convictions, shall be adjudged an habitual criminal.***

(e) Except when the death penalty is imposed, anyone adjudged an habitual criminal shall be sentenced to life imprisonment.

E. Critical Thinking

►Do the classifications for the offenses of theft and burglary seem consistent with one another? Explain your answer.

►Is the habitual offender statute necessary? Do you feel the judge should have the discretion to impose a lighter sentence?

►Under what circumstances might a "fine only" be a more appropriate sentence for a defendant than incarceration?

F. Case

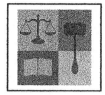

In the following case the defendant, Vaughn Washington, was indicted for the murder of Rudy Jones, the attempted murder of Leroy Martin, a police officer, armed violence against Jones and Martin, and unlawful use of weapons. The trial court found the defendant guilty of murder and armed violence. Defendant was sentenced to a term of natural life. Washington appealed his convictions raising several issues on appeal including: whether attempted murder may be used as a predicate offense for a finding of habitual criminality; whether the habitual criminal statute is unconstitutional; and whether the trial judge violated the habitual offender statute.

PEOPLE v. WASHINGTON
125 Ill.App.3d 109, 80 Ill.Dec. 554, 465 N.E.2d 666 (1 Dist. 1984)

[Case citations omitted.]

BACKGROUND

Justice JOHNSON delivered the opinion of the court:

…Defendant had previously been convicted of attempted murder and armed robbery. Defendant claims that attempted murder is not a Class X felony because the statute provides that the sentence for attempted murder "is the sentence for a Class X felony." (Ill.Rev.Stat.1981, ch. 38, par. 8-4(c)(1).) Other Class X statutes provide that the offense "is a Class X felony." (See, for example, Ill.Rev.Stat.1981, ch. 38, par. 11-1(c).) Defendant contends that the difference in language suggests that the legislature did not intend that attempted murder be treated as a Class X felony for all purposes. Alternatively, defendant argues that even if attempted murder is a Class X felony, under *ex post facto* principles, this court should consider the attempt statute at the time the offense was committed. Previously, attempted murder had the sentence for a Class 1 felony. Ill.Rev.Stat. 1975, ch. 38, par. 8-4(c)(1).

…We reject defendant's argument…we hold that the trial court properly invoked the habitual criminal statute where defendant had previously been convicted of attempted murder and armed robbery, both offenses now classified as Class X felonies.

Defendant offers several arguments that the habitual criminal statute is unconstitutional. First, defendant claims that the statute does not provide adequate notice to a defendant that if he is convicted the prosecutor will seek a natural life sentence. The prosecutor may wait until the sentencing hearing before giving such notice. According to defendant, this deficiency in the statutory notice requirement and the lateness of notice violates the due process clauses of the United States and Illinois constitutions. Defendant contends that notice is required well in advance of the sentencing hearing so that the defendant's attorney will have time to challenge prior convictions so as to uncover any infirmity. Defendant also claims that by failing to require the State to prove beyond a reasonable doubt the existence of facts requiring the enhanced penalty, the habitual criminal statute violates the rule of *People v. Ostrand* as modified in *People v. Hayes.*

...We reject defendant's argument. The habitual criminal statute is concerned with sentencing. When defendant was charged with murder, he was put on notice that if convicted he would be subject to all possible penalties applicable to such a conviction. ...[T]he Supreme Court [has] held that due process does not require advance notice that the trial on the substantive offense will be followed by a habitual criminal proceeding, although a defendant must receive reasonable notice and an opportunity to be heard relative to the recidivist charge. In the instant case, defendant had an adequate opportunity to prepare a possible defense to invocation of the habitual criminal statute. Defendant was found guilty of murder on December 15, 1981. The sentencing hearing was held on January 12, 1982. At the hearing, the trial court asked defendant's attorney whether he wanted to rebut the *prima facie* presumption of validity established by certified copies of defendant's prior convictions for armed robbery and attempted murder. The attorney stated that he had nothing to rebut the presumption. We hold that defendant waived his right to challenge the validity of his prior convictions.***

Defendant argues that the habitual criminal statute removes all of the sentencing authority traditionally reserved to judges and gives it to the prosecutor. The statute gives the prosecutor absolute discretion as to whom he wishes to sentence to life imprisonment, and gives the prosecutor no standards or other guidance in making this decision, allowing him at his whim to sentence one person to spend the rest of his life in prison while another serves only a term of years. The statute violates the separation of powers doctrine by taking the sentencing function from the judicial branch and giving it to the executive branch by a legislative infringement of an exclusively judicial function, and by improperly delegating legislative power to the executive branch. Defendant contends that the habitual criminal statute should either be declared unconstitutional or construed as nonmandatory.

...The issues of whether the habitual criminal statute is unconstitutional because it gives the prosecution unbridled discretion in deciding whether to seek the imposition of a life sentence and because it violates the separation of powers doctrine have been addressed [in other cases; in one]...the court stated that the language in the habitual criminal statute "does not explicitly delegate to the State the power to choose which defendants shall be made subject to its terms. Rather, its provisions apply to 'every person' who meets its criteria. The word 'may' in section 33B-2(a) can be read as prescribing how the prosecutor brings to the court's attention a defendant's prior conviction history." [In another case]...the court concluded that the habitual criminal provision did not violate the separation of powers doctrine. Therefore, we conclude that the habitual criminal statute is not unconstitutional as granting unbridled discretion to the prosecutor or as violative of the separation of powers doctrine.

...Next, defendant argues that the habitual criminal statute is unconstitutional because it requires the imposition of natural life imprisonment while forbidding consideration of personal characteristics and the seriousness of the offense, thus violating the Illinois Constitution, due process, and the eighth amendment to the United States Constitution. A similar argument was considered at length but rejected in [a previous case]. Accordingly, we hold that the habitual criminal statute does not violate the Illinois Constitution, due process, nor the eighth amendment to the United States Constitution.

Defendant contends that the habitual criminal statute violates the United States and Illinois constitutional provisions regarding *ex post facto* laws and double jeopardy. He claims that under the statute, a defendant is punished not just for committing the third offense but for being a habitual criminal. Thus, he is necessarily being punished for the two earlier offenses which made up part of the finding of habitual criminality. Since this punishment was in part for offenses committed prior to the effective date of the habitual criminal statute, the *ex post facto* principle is violated. The double jeopardy provision is violated because defendant is being punished a second time for the first two offenses which are alleged as part of the charge of habitual criminality.

...We again reject defendant's arguments. Recidivist statutes have been consistently upheld as not violative of *ex post facto* constitutional provisions.... Under the habitual criminal statute, defendant is not punished a second time for a prior offense; rather, prior adjudications are used to establish matters in aggravation to support the disposition authorized for a third serious offense.... Accordingly, we hold that the habitual criminal statute does not violate *ex post facto* and double jeopardy provisions of the Illinois and United States constitutions.

Defendant argues that he was denied his statutory and due process right to a hearing at which the State must prove defendant's prior convictions. He alleges that the trial judge failed to directly address and inform him of his right to a habitual offender hearing and improperly allowed defense counsel to waive his right to a hearing even though counsel had not consulted with him. Defendant claims it was error to shift to him the burden of disputing the convictions.

...Defendant's argument has no merit. When defendant was pronounced guilty, he was put on notice that a sentencing hearing would follow. As we stated above, defendant waived his right to challenge the validity of his prior convictions at the sentencing hearing. Moreover, at the hearing, defendant said that he "did all of those things in the past," thus admitting the validity of his past convictions. Therefore, we hold that defendant was not deprived of his right to a habitual offender hearing.

***

G. Questions:

Please choose the correct answer for the following questions.

1. An offense for which an sentence to a term of imprisonment for less than one year is a:

a. felony
b. misdemeanor
c. business offense
d. petty offense

2. For a Class C misdemeanor, a sentence of imprisonment may not exceed:

a. 5 years
b. 1 year
c. 6 months
d. 30 days

3. Enhanced penalties may be imposed based upon:

a. the specific conduct of the defendant
b. subsequent convictions
c. both a and b
d. neither a nor b

4. In Illinois, theft is classified as a:

a. felony or misdemeanor
b. felony only
c. misdemeanor only
d. business offense

5. In Illinois, burglary is classified as a:

a. felony or misdemeanor
b. felony only
c. misdemeanor only
d. business offense

CHAPTER TWO

Constitutional Limits on Criminal Law

Each state has its own constitution. While Illinois first adopted its Constitution in 1818, the present version of the Illinois Constitution was adopted in 1970. Article I of the Illinois Constitution contains a Bill of Rights. When first adopted, the Bill of Rights contained in the U.S. Constitution afforded rights to individuals only on the federal level. Over the last half of the twentieth century the U.S. Supreme Court has held most of the fundamental rights found in the first ten amendments applicable to the states.

Article II of the Illinois Constitution provides for three branches of government in Illinois: legislative, executive and judicial. Following the U.S. Constitution, the Illinois Constitution provides for separation of powers ensuring that no one branch will have absolute power over an individual charged with a crime.

Article IV places legislative power in a General Assembly which consists of a Senate and a House of Representatives. Article V grants supreme executive power to the Governor. Judicial power is vested in a Supreme Court, an Appellate Court and Circuit Courts in Article VI.

I. Freedom of Speech, Right to Assemble and Petition

A. Comments

As discussed in Chapter 1, our laws are defined in the Illinois Compiled Statutes. While constitutional law does not define offenses, it does set limits on what conduct may be deemed criminal and the sanction which may be imposed for that conduct, as well as the procedures used in criminal investigations and prosecutions. While the Illinois Constitution is supreme within this state, it may not conflict with a federal law or the U.S. Constitution. Should a law passed by the General Assembly be found to violate the right of an individual as provided in either the Illinois Constitution or the U.S. Constitution, it cannot be enforced. A state constitution may, however, provide more expansive individual liberties than those granted by the U.S. Constitution. At times, the Illinois Supreme Court has conducted an independent analysis of the Illinois Constitution and found that certain provisions offer greater protection than those afforded by similar rights under the Federal Constitution.

The Bill of Rights found in Article I of the Illinois Constitution differs from the first ten amendments of the U.S. Constitution in many respects. Some differences are more significant than others. The fundamental freedoms of speech, assembly and petition on the federal and state levels appear below.

B. Constitutional Provisions

U.S. Constitution – Amendment I

Congress shall make no law respecting an establishment of religion, or prohibiting the free exercise thereof; or abridging the freedom of speech, or of the press, or the right of the people peaceably to assemble, and to petition the Government for a redress of grievances.

Constitution of the State of Illinois

Section 4. FREEDOM OF SPEECH. All persons may speak, write and publish freely, being responsible for the abuse of that liberty. In trials for libel, both civil and criminal, the truth when published with good motives and for justifiable ends, shall be a sufficient defense.

Section 6. RIGHT TO ASSEMBLE AND PETITION. The people have the right to assemble in a peaceable manner, to consult for the common good, to make known their opinions to their representatives and to apply for redress of grievances.

C. Constitutional Issue: Flag Desecration

In 1989, the U.S. Supreme Court decided the case of *Texas v. Johnson,* 491 U.S. 397, 109 S.Ct. 2533, 105 L.Ed.2d 342. The case arose from an incident which took place outside the Republican National Convention held in Dallas in 1984. Johnson took part in a political demonstration protesting the policies of the Reagan administration. Following a march through the streets, Johnson burned an American flag while protesters chanted. While no one was threatened or injured, several witnesses stated they were seriously offended by the burning of the flag. Johnson was convicted under a Texas statute for desecration of a venerated object.

The case was eventually heard by the Supreme Court. The Court held, in part, that Johnson's burning of the flag constituted expressive conduct and therefore, his conviction for flag desecration was inconsistent with the First Amendment. While the First Amendment refers specifically to "speech," the Court noted that it has long recognized that First Amendment protection does not end at the spoken or written word. While some of the justices were obviously disturbed by Johnson's actions, the majority opinion states, "[t]he government may not prohibit the verbal or nonverbal expression of an idea merely because society finds the idea offensive or disagreeable even where our flag is involved." The Court pointed out that a state many not foster its own view of the flag by prohibiting expressive conduct relating to it.

D. Illinois Statute

720 ILCS 620/1 Flag desecration prohibited

Sec. 1. Any person who (a) for exhibition or display, places or causes to be placed any word, figure, mark, picture, design, drawing, or any advertisement of any nature, upon any flag, standard, color or ensign of the United States or State flag of this State or ensign, (b) exposes or causes to be exposed to public view any such flag, standard, color or ensign, upon which has been printed, painted or otherwise placed, or to which has been attached, appended, affixed, or annexed, any word, figure, mark, picture, design or drawing or any advertisement of any nature, or (c) exposes to public view, manufactures, sells, exposes for sale, gives away, or has in possession for sale or to give away or for use for any purpose, any article or substance, being an article of merchandise, or a receptacle of merchandise or article or thing for carrying or transporting merchandise upon which has been printed, painted, attached, or otherwise placed a representation of any such flag, standard, color, or ensign, to advertise, call attention to, decorate, mark or distinguish the article or substance on which so placed, shall be guilty of a Class C misdemeanor.

Any person who publicly mutilates, defaces, defiles, tramples, or intentionally displays on the ground or floor any such flag, standard, color or ensign shall be guilty of a Class 4 felony.

E. Critical Thinking

►On its face, does the Illinois statute appear to infringe on an individual's freedom of expression?

►Considering the Supreme Court's holding in *Texas v. Johnson,* make an argument as to whether or not the Illinois statute prohibiting flag desecration is constitutional. Have your personal feelings on the issue of flag burning entered into your argument?

F. Case

Defendants were charged, in separate prosecutions, with knowingly transmitting human immunodeficiency virus (HIV) to another person through intimate contact. Two circuit courts declared the criminal statute under which the defendants were charged to be unconstitutional. The cases were consolidated for appeal.

PEOPLE v. RUSSELL
PEOPLE v. LUNSFORD
158 Ill.2d 23, 196 Ill.Dec. 629, 630 N.E.2d 794, (1994)
cert. denied, 513 U.S. 828, 115 S.Ct. 97, 130 L.Ed.2d 47

[Case citations omitted.]

Justice HEIPLE delivered the opinion of the court:

In 1989, the Illinois General Assembly made it a crime for a knowing carrier of the HIV virus to transmit this virus to another person through intimate contact. The stated offense is designated as a Class 2 felony which, though subject to probation, carries a possible sentence of imprisonment from three to seven years. We take judicial notice of the fact that the HIV virus is a precursor to AIDS, a progressive and inevitably fatal disease syndrome. We further take judicial notice of the fact that intimate sexual contact whereby blood or semen of an infected person is transferred to an uninfected person is a primary method of spreading the infection.

Neither of the court orders below indicates whether the statute is violative of either the State or Federal Constitutions. No article, section or clause of either constitution is alluded to. It could be the Constitution of the United States. It could be that of Illinois. It could be both. We are left to surmise which constitution or which portion thereof the trial judges may have had in mind.

From the defendants/appellees' briefs, however, we are informed that both the Federal and State Constitutions are allegedly violated by the statute for reasons of free speech and association (U.S. Const., amend. I; Ill. Const.1970, art. I, §§ 4, 5); and that the statute is so vague as to deny the defendants due process of law. (U.S. Const., amend. V; Ill. Const.1970, art. I, § 2.) These arguments are without merit.

In one of the cases before us, the criminal complaint charges that the defendant Caretha Russell knew that she was infected with the HIV virus when she engaged in consensual sexual intercourse with [another] without telling [him] of her infection. In the other case, defendant Timothy Lunsford is charged with raping a woman at a time when he knew he was infected with the HIV virus.

Neither the statute nor the cases before us have even the slightest connection with free speech. Consequently, pursuant to constitutional interpretations of the United States Supreme Court, defendants' overbreadth argument and their argument of facial vagueness are inapplicable.

Additionally, the defendants' cases do not infringe on any supposed right of intimate association as claimed. In fact, we know of no such right. The facts are that in the first of the two cases, the victim did not know that his sexual partner had HIV. In the second of the two cases, the HIV transmission charge is appendant to a charge of forcible rape. It is preposterous to argue that the statute constitutes a violation of either of the defendants' supposed right to intimate association in these situations. Finally, the vagueness argument is in error both facially and factually. Reference to the specific language of the statute makes this clear.

The subject statute provides in pertinent part:
Criminal Transmission of HIV. (a) A person commits criminal transmission of HIV when he or she, knowing that he or she is infected with HIV:
(1) engages in intimate contact with another;***

(b) For purposes of this Section:***
'Intimate contact with another' means the exposure of the body of one person to a bodily fluid of another person in a manner that could result in the transmission of HIV."
720 ILCS 5/12-16.2

Vagueness, like beauty, may be in the eye of the beholder. We, however, read the statute as being sufficiently clear and explicit so that a person of ordinary intelligence need not have to guess at its meaning or application. Also, it provides sufficiently definite standards for law enforcement officers and triers of fact so that its application need not depend merely on their private conceptions.

That the statute might open the innocent conduct of others to possible prosecution is a matter of pure speculation and conjecture which is not before us in these consolidated cases. We are here concerned only with the specific conduct of these defendants and the application of the statute to them.

For the foregoing reasons, we hold that the statute in question is not violative of either the Illinois or the United States Constitution. Accordingly, we reverse the judgments of the courts below and remand these causes for further proceedings.

G. Critical Thinking

▶Do you agree with the conclusion of the Illinois Supreme Court that a "person of ordinary intelligence" can understand the meaning and application of the statute defining Criminal Transmission of HIV? Explain your answer.

H. Case

The defendant in this case was convicted of criminal trespass to land for handing out political material on Dominick's property. The question is whether his activities were protected under the constitution of the United States and the Illinois Constitution.

PEOPLE v. DIGUIDA
152 Ill.2d 104, 178 Ill.Dec. 80, 604 N.E.2d 336 (1992)

Case citations omitted.

Justice MORAN delivered the opinion of the court:

Defendant, Paul DiGuida, was convicted of criminal trespass to real property after refusing to leave the premises of a grocery store where he had been soliciting signatures for a political petition. Defendant appealed his conviction. The appellate court reversed his conviction holding that while his activities were not protected under the first amendment of the U.S. Constitution, they were protected by the free speech and free and equal elections provisions of the Illinois Constitution. Because this case presents a question under the Illinois Constitution which arose for the first time as a result of the appellate court's decision, we accepted the State's petition to appeal as a matter of right.

The issue presented for review is whether a private store's invocation of the criminal trespass to land statute, in order to exclude a circulator of a political nominating petition from its premises, is violative of the free speech and free elections provisions of the Illinois Constitution of 1970 (Ill. Const. 1970, art. I, §§ 2, 4; art. III, § 3). This is a question of first impression for this court.

BACKGROUND

On December 12, 1987, defendant was standing inside the cart-control area of a Dominick's grocery store in Evanston, gathering signatures on a nominating petition for a Cook County political candidate. The cart-control area, located between the store entrance and the public sidewalk, is owned by Dominick's. It is covered by an overhand and surrounded by a railing which prevents carts from rolling into the parking lot. Defendant was standing on Dominick's property, approximately 25 feet from the entranced, when Ted Scanlon, a store manager, approached defendant and asked him to leave. Scanlon explained that Dominick's did not allow soliciting on its property. Defendant responded that he did not have to leave, as he was on public property, and could do what he wanted. Scanlon informed defendant that he would call the police if defendant did not leave. Defendant told Scanlon to go ahead, as he was doing nothing wrong. According to his own testimony, defendant then walked around the block in order to avoid the police. After the police had left, defendant returned to the cart-control area and continued to solicit signatures. The police returned, informed defendant that he was on private property, and told him that he would be arrested if he did not leave. Defendant refused to leave. He was then arrested and charged in a misdemeanor complaint with criminal trespass to land. At the conclusion of trial, the court found defendant guilty of criminal trespass to land, holding that his first amendment rights were curtailed on private property.***

FREE SPEECH PROVISION OF THE ILLINOIS CONSTITUTION

Although defendant acknowledges that the Federal Constitution did not shield his expressive activities, he contends that the more liberal provisions of the Illinois Constitution gave him the right to solicit political signatures at Dominick's. Various *amici curiae* join defendant in urging that we abandon what has been termed the "lockstep doctrine." Under this doctrine the court would consistently apply decisions of the United States Supreme Court based on Federal constitutional provisions to the construction of comparable provisions of the State constitution. However, this court has not found itself bound in every case requiring State constitutional construction by doctrine derived from Supreme Court interpretation of the Constitution of the United States. Rather, the court has looked to the intent behind our constitution in order to determine whether comparable provisions should receive a similar interpretation. As this court has previously stated, where the language of the State constitution, or where debates and committee reports of the constitutional convention show that the Framers intended a different construction, it will construe similar provisions in a different way from that of the Supreme Court.***

The court has found that the Illinois Constitution's guarantee of due process to all persons (Ill. Const. 1970, art. I, § 2) stands separate and independent from the Federal guarantee of due process. …[T]his court has at various times conducted an independent analysis of the Illinois Constitution and found that certain provisions offer our citizens greater protection than that enjoyed under the United States Constitution.***

The first amendment [of the U.S. Constitution]…specifically limits the powers of government, not that of private persons. By contrast, article I, section 4, of the Illinois Constitution does not expressly restrict its application to governmental interference. However, other provisions of the Illinois Constitution have consistently been interpreted as providing protection only against interference by the government, despite the lack of specific wording to that effect. This court has found, for instance, that the due process and equal protection provisions of the Illinois Constitution, as well as section 6 of article I, which creates a right of freedom from invasion of privacy, apply only to actions by government or public officials.***

After considering proceedings of the Illinois Constitutional Convention of 1970, past decisions of this court, the decisions of other jurisdictions, and generally accepted doctrine concerning the reach of constitutional provisions, we conclude that article I, section 4, of the Illinois Constitution of 1970 was not intended to apply to actions taken by private persons, but only to actions by the State. Such a requirement of State action is necessary in order to preserve the private autonomy of our citizens.

Having determined that State action is required to bring into play the free speech protections of the constitution, our next inquiry is whether that element exists in the case before us. The appellate court below found that use of the criminal trespass law constituted State action.***

...[D]efendant was not arrested because of the content of his speech or prosecuted because of his expressive activities. He was arrested and prosecuted simply because he refused to leave Dominick's property. The State action in this case was directed exclusively at enforcing the trespass law. Only indirectly did it interfere with defendant's right to free expression.***

We have concluded that an individual's constitutional right to free expression is effective only against public or quasi-public entities, and that use of the criminal trespass to land law does not constitute State action. Thus, whether defendant's speech was constitutionally protected becomes a question of whether Dominick's itself had taken on such a public aspect that it became a forum for free expression.***

...[A] finding that the State constitution gives greater rights of free expression than the Federal Constitution to persons on the premises of a free-standing private store might well be found unconstitutional by the Supreme Court. However, it is not necessary to anticipate that this court's decision will conflict with Federal law. We conclude that the Dominick's store in this case was not a public or quasi-public establishment, and that consequently its exclusion of defendant did not violate article I, section 4, of the Illinois Constitution.

***

II. Doctrines of Vagueness and Overbreadth

A. Comments

Whether a state statute is constitutional is a matter of law. While there is a strong presumption that a statute is constitutional, a defendant may rebut that presumption. Due process requires that a criminal statute be clearly defined. If a contested statute involves a first amendment right, the defendant may argue that the statute is impermissibly vague as applied to himself and that the statute is unconstitutional as written because it might be vague as applied to another. Besides ensuring that a person of reasonable intelligence can understand the meaning and application of the law, the vagueness doctrine means to limit the discretion of law enforcement officers and prosecutors in enforcing statutes.

A defendant may argue the constitutionality of a statute involving first amendment expressive rights under the doctrine of overbreadth. The purpose of the doctrine is to protect an individual's first amendment freedom of expression from laws written so broadly that the fear of punishment might discourage people from taking advantage of that freedom.

B. Statute

720 ILCS 5/25-1.1 Unlawful contact with streetgang members reads in relevant part as follows:

(a) A person commits the offense of unlawful contact with streetgang members when:

(1) He or she knowingly has direct or indirect contact with a streetgang member as defined in Section 10 of the Illinois Streetgang Terrorism Omnibus Prevention Act after having been sentenced to...supervision for a criminal offense with a condition of such sentence being to refrain from direct or indirect contact with a streetgang member or members[.]

C. Case

The defendant appealed his conviction for unlawful contact with a street gang member. He contends the statute under which he was convicted is unconstitutionally vague and overbroad. The appellate court disagreed.

PEOPLE v. JAMESSON
329 Ill.App.3d 446, 263 Ill.Dec. 736, 768 N.E.2d 817 (2 Dist. 2002)

[Case citations omitted.]

PRESIDING JUSTICE HUTCHINSON delivered the opinion of the court:

Bryce Jamesson was convicted of the offense of unlawful contact with a street gang member and was sentenced to two years' probation. Just prior to this charge being filed, the defendant had plead guilty to the offense of possession of cannabis and had been sentenced to a term of six months' court supervision and as a condition of supervision, he was to have no contact with [a specific individual] or any other known gang members. As part of defendant's appeal on his most recent conviction, he challenged the constitutionality of the statute under which he was charged and convicted.

We will first address the constitutionality of the statute under which defendant was charged and convicted because, in the event that the statute at issue is declared unconstitutional on its face, the ultimate outcome would be to vacate defendant's conviction based upon that statute.

***

A law can be facially unconstitutional under two different theories. First, laws that inhibit the exercise of first amendment rights can be invalidated under the over breadth doctrine....Second, a law can be found to be impermissibly vague, even if it does not reach a substantial amount of constitutionally protected conduct, if it fails to define the offense with sufficient definiteness that ordinary people can understand what conduct is prohibited and it fails to establish standards to permit enforcement in a nonarbitrary, nondiscriminatory manner....

...[D]efendant contends that the unlawful-contact statute is facially overbroad and, therefore, unconstitutional because it fails to contain a mental state element beyond passive contact with another citizen. Because the statute exposes an accused to punishment for innocent contact with others, defendant concludes that the statute violates a citizen's right to free assembly.

The doctrine of overbreadth was designed to protect first amendment freedom of expression from laws written so broadly the fear of punishment might discourage taking advantage of that freedom....A statute regulating conduct is overly broad if it (1) criminalizes a substantial amount of protected behavior, relative to the law's plainly legitimate sweep, and (2) is not susceptible to a limiting construction that avoids constitutional problems....The overbreadth doctrine should be employed sparingly and only when a challenger can prove that a statute's overbreadth is real and substantial....

In the present case, we reject defendant's argument that the statute can be applied to innocent or constitutionally protected conduct. While the offense of unlawful contact with street gang members does contain an element of association, this type of association does not fall within the ambit of the first amendment. Where the association is an integral part of the unlawful conduct, it has no constitutional protection....Here, the trial court imposed a limitation on defendant's association with others as a part of a valid criminal sentence....The element of association in the unlawful contact statute is an integral part of the offense. The offense cannot be committed without the prior condition of supervision, a gathering of street gang members, and defendant's knowing decision to place himself within the assemblage of those street gang members. Therefore, the element of association in the unlawful contact with street gang members is not constitutionally protected.

Moreover, the unlawful-contact statute is directed only at that type of knowing contact that is unlawful. Defendant was not issued a complaint because he happened to be in close proximity to two other Latin Count gang members while waiting for a ride from someone named Robert. Rather, defendant was issued a complaint because [the officer] recognized defendant in the company of two known gang members; [the officer] knew defendant had just been sentenced to a term of supervision based upon a criminal offense; [the officer] knew that the trial court had ordered defendant to have no contact with street gang members....

Contrary to defendant's assertion, section 25-1.1 does not lack a mental state element. Section 25-1.1 expressly provides that the mental state for the offense of unlawful contact with street gang members is knowledge. A person may be convicted under this statute only if that person knowingly and unlawfully violates a specific court sentencing order. Any other individual who has not been the subject of a criminal prosecution and who has not been specifically ordered in a sentencing decree to avoid knowing contact with street gang members is clearly not subject to punishment under this statute...Therefore, no person could reasonably believe that punishment would be real and substantial for any conduct not in violation of a specific court order. We conclude that the Illinois criminal offense of unlawful contact with street gang members is not unconstitutionally overbroad.

We next address defendant's contention that the unlawful-contact statute is unconstitutionally vague because the term "contact" is a concept about which reasonable people will have to speculate to give meaning. A facial challenge to determine whether a statute is impermissibly vague is limited...To prevail on a vagueness challenge to a statute that does not implicate first amendment concerns, as is the case here, a party must demonstrate that the statute was vague as applied to the conduct for which the party is being prosecuted...Due process requires that a statute not be so vague that person of common intelligence must necessarily guess at its meaning or application...The determination of whether a statute is void for vagueness must be made in the factual context of each case.***

In the present case, we determine that the unlawful-contact statute is not vague. We recognize that criminal acts cannot always be defined with absolute precision...The word "contact" bears definitions of "association, relationship," "connection, communication," and "to get in communication with." See Webster's Ninth New Collegiate Dictionary 282 (1990). Section 25-1.1 of the Criminal Code requires a defendant to knowingly have contact with a gang member, despite an explicit prohibition in a trial court's sentencing order, for a violation to occur...We believe that a person of ordinary intelligence would reasonably know that she or he could not knowingly communicate with, meet with, or associate with those gang members as set out in the sentencing order. Moreover, trial courts have long used their discretion to impose "no contact" conditions in imposing sentences.***

Inasmuch as defendant is the party challenging the constitutionality of a statute, he bears the burden of clearly establishing the constitutional violation...Upon our review of the issues presented, we determine that defendant has failed to satisfy that burden.***

D. Critical Thinking

▶ What is your opinion as to the legitimacy of defendant's challenge to the Illinois statute based upon the doctrines of vagueness and overbreadth?

► How do these doctrines compare with the concept of 'ignorance of the law is no excuse'?

III. Crime Victims

A. Comments

Since 1970, three amendments have been added to the Illinois Constitution's Bill of Rights. In 1992 Illinois voters adopted at general election what is now Article I, Section 8.1 affording victims of crime certain rights. With the growing concern for how victims are treated within the criminal justice system, most states have adopted such amendments. Although crime victims' rights amendments have been proposed on the federal level, the U.S. Constitution does not yet include such rights.

B. Illinois Constitution - Crime Victim's Rights

SECTION 8.1. CRIME VICTIM'S RIGHTS. (a) Crime victims, as defined by law, shall have the following rights as provided by law: (1) The right to be treated with fairness and respect for their dignity and privacy throughout the criminal justice process. (2) The right to notification of court proceedings. (3) The right to communicate with the prosecution. (4) The right to make a statement to the court at sentencing. (5) The right to information about the conviction, sentence, imprisonment, and release of the accused. (6) The right to timely disposition of the case following the arrest of the accused. (7) The right to be reasonably protected from the accused throughout the criminal justice process. (8) The right to be present at the trial and all other court proceedings on the same basis as the accused, unless the victim is to testify and the court determines that the victim's testimony would be materially affected if the victim hears other testimony at the trial. (9) The right to have present at all court proceedings, subject to the rules of evidence, an advocate or other support person of the victim's choice. (10) The right to restitution. (b) The General Assembly may provide by law for the enforcement of this Section. (c) The General Assembly may provide for an assessment against convicted defendants to pay for crime victims' rights. (d) Nothing in this Section or in any law enacted under this Section shall be construed as creating a basis for vacating a conviction or a ground for appellate relief in any criminal case.

C. Critical Thinking

▶ Make an argument for, or against, a victims' rights amendment to the U.S. Constitution.

▶ How do the rights afforded crime victims in Article I, Section 8.1 of the Illinois Constitution compare with the protections found in the Bill of Rights granted to defendants? Has Section 8.1 gone far enough? Has it gone too far?

D. Web Activity

For an example of services provided to crime victims, visit the DuPage County State's Attorneys Office site at the following URL:

▶ http://www.dupageco.org/statesattorney/generic.cfm?doc_id=215

E. Questions

Please choose the correct answer for the following questions.

1. Which of the following is a true statement regarding the Illinois Constitution?

a. the most recent version was adopted in 1970
b. The Bill of Rights is identical to that of the U.S. Constitution
c. it provides for two primary branches of government
d. it defines Illinois criminal laws

2. Individuals have a constitutional right to:

a. assemble and petition
b. free expression
c. intimate association
d. a and b only

3. A defendant may argue that a statute is unconstitutionally vague:

a. as to himself
b. as to another
c. both a and be
d. neither a nor b

4. Since 1970, the Illinois Constitution has:

a. remained the same
b. had 3 amendments added to the Bill of Rights
c. undergone a complete revision
d. none of the above

5. In Illinois, crime victim's rights are:

a. outlined in the statutes
b. found in the Illinois Constitution
c. identical to victim's rights in the U.S. Constitution
d. all of the above

CHAPTER THREE

The Criminal Act

Most violations of the criminal law require a voluntary act as well as the intent to commit a crime. The criminal act is known as *actus reus* (pronounced *ak*-tus *ray*-us). The intent to commit a crime is known as *mens rea* (pronounced *mehns* ray-ah). This Chapter will focus on the criminal act.

It is not a crime to merely think about violating the law. Besides being unconstitutional, and virtually impossible to prove, it does no harm to society. Generally, criminal laws require a concurrence between the *actus reus* and *mens rea*.

The criminal act required in Illinois is addressed in the following statute:

720 ILCS 5/4-1 Voluntary act
A material element of every offense is a voluntary act, which includes an omission to perform a duty which the law imposes on the offender and which he is physically capable of performing.

For purposes of criminal law, a person will not be sanctioned for failure to perform a moral duty. However, a legal duty to act may occur based upon:

1) a duty established by statute,
2) a contractual duty, or
3) a special relationship of the actor to the victim.

In Illinois for example, a sex offender has a statutory duty to register with the Department of State Police. An individual working as a lifeguard has a contractual duty to rescue a swimmer in trouble. Special relationships requiring a legal duty include those between a parent and child and that of a caregiver to the elderly.

I. Failure to Act

A. Comments

Note that the Illinois statute defining a voluntary act includes a failure to act. An omission, or failure to act, constitutes the *actus reus* when that person has a legal duty to perform some act under certain circumstances. Consider the following Illinois laws creating a legal duty to act based upon the special relationship between the actor and the victim.

B. Statutes

720 ILCS 5/12-21.5 Child Abandonment

(a) A person commits the offense of child abandonment when he or she, as a parent, guardian, or other person having physical custody or control of a child, without regard for the mental or physical health, safety, or welfare of that child, knowingly leaves that child who is under the age of 13 without supervision by a responsible person over the age of 14 for a period of 24 hours or more.***

(d) Child abandonment is a Class 4 felony. A second or subsequent offense after a prior conviction is a Class 3 felony.***

720 ILCS 5/12-21.6 Endangering the life or health of a child

(a) It is unlawful for any person to willfully cause or permit the life or health of a child under the age of 18 to be endangered or to willfully cause or permit a child to be placed in circumstances that endanger the child's life or health.***

(d) A violation of this Section is a Class A misdemeanor. A second or subsequent violation of this Section is a Class 3 felony. A violation of this Section that is a proximate cause of the death of the child is a Class 3 felony for which a person, if sentenced to a term of imprisonment, shall be sentenced to a term of not less than 2 years and not more than 10 years.

720 ILCS 5/12-21 Criminal abuse or neglect of an elderly or disabled person

(a) A person commits the offense of criminal abuse or neglect of an elderly or disabled person when he or she is a caregiver and he or she knowingly:
(1) performs acts that cause the elderly or disabled person's life to be endangered, health to be injured, or pre-existing physical or mental condition to deteriorate; or
(2) fails to perform acts that he or she knows or reasonably should know are necessary to maintain or preserve the life or health of the elderly or disabled person and such failure causes the elderly or disabled person's life to be endangered, health to be injured or pre-existing physical or mental condition to deteriorate; or
(3) abandons the elderly or disabled person; or
(4) physically abuses, harasses, intimidates, or interferes with the personal liberty of the elderly or disabled person or exposes the elderly or disabled person to willful deprivation.
Criminal abuse or neglect of an elderly or disabled person is a Class 3 felony.

C. Case

The following case is an example of the legal duty which exists between a caregiver and an elderly or disabled person. The facts of this case provide good reason for why the law exists.

PEOPLE v. JANICE SIMESTER and DALE SIMESTER
287 Ill.App.3d 420, 222 Ill.Dec. 838, 678 N.E.2d 710 (1 Dist. 1997)

[Case citations omitted.]

After a jury trial, defendants Janice and Dale Simester, who are married, were each convicted of two counts of criminal neglect of an elderly person [720 ILCS 5/12-21] and sentenced to 30 months' probation and 1,000 hours of community service.

***

At trial, the evidence established that defendant Janice Simester lived in the same household with her codefendant Dale Simester, their two young children and the victim, her 74-year-old uncle Stanley Pierzga, who had lived with her and her parents for over 20 years. When Janice's parents died, she continued to live with and care for her uncle in her parents' home.

…[A] paramedic with the Oak Forest Fire Department, testified that at 7:58 p.m. on August 10, 1993, he was called to defendants' home. Janice answered the door and told him that the victim was upstairs. [He] immediately noticed a strong smell coming from the house and, whole proceeding upstairs, the smell became much stronger. He entered the victim's bedroom where he found him lying on the floor in a fetal position. The victim and his bedroom were filthy. The victim's clothes, hands, bedding, floor and television were covered with feces. His clothes were also urine soaked. After checking the victim's vital signs, [he] shook him but was unable to get a response. When he attempted to roll the victim onto his back, the victim's clothing stuck to the floor. The victim remained in a rigid fetal position even after he had been placed on his back.

***

Dale Simester testified that after both of his wife's parents died, Janice was responsible for the care of her uncle, the victim, while he, Dale, had no responsibility for his care. He testified that the victim would not even allow him to come into his room. He stated that he saw the victim on August 4, 1993, before he left for a three-day golf outing. He did not see the victim again until the day of the incident. On that day, Janice told him that the victim had fallen, and he heard the victim tell her to leave him alone. Later in the evening, Janice told him that she checked on the victim, found that he was having trouble breathing and was going to call a doctor. Dale admitted that although he knew that the victim had fallen at approximately 5 p.m., he and his wife left the house to pick up their children and did not check on him again until after 7 p.m.

Janice Simester testified that while her husband was away on his golf outing, she had no one to help her with her household duties and, as a result, she did not check on the victim as much as she should have. She further stated that until the day of the incident, she believed that the victim was in good health.... She also stated that on the day of the incident she went up to the victim's room after she arrived home from work. When she knocked on the door, the victim was "hollering." She found that the victim had fallen, but he told her that he could get up by himself. She noted that the bed sheets were soiled, so she stripped his bed. After leaving the victim in order to pick up her children from day care, she returned to find him still lying on the bedroom floor. She further stated that when she first observed him on the floor, she did not observe the feces on his body and clothing.

***

The statute defines "caregiver" as a person who has a duty to provide for an elderly person's health and personal care at the person's place of residence, including but not limited to food and nutrition, shelter, hygiene, prescribed medication and medical care and treatment. The statute provides that the term "caregiver" shall include:

> "a parent, spouse, adult child or other relative by blood or marriage who resides with or resides in the same building with and regularly visits the elderly or disabled person, knows or reasonably should know of such person's physical or mental impairment and knows or reasonably should know that such person is unable to adequately provide for his own health and personal care."

***

...[W]e find that the evidence overwhelmingly demonstrated that defendants were guilty beyond a reasonable doubt. The evidence established that the defendants were the victim's caregivers as contemplated by the statute. We specifically note that although Dale protests that he had no responsibilities for the victim's care and thus cannot be culpable under the statute as a "caregiver," he clearly falls within the language of the statute defining a caregiver as a *"relative by* ****marriage who resides with* or resides in the same building with and regularly visits *the elderly or disabled person."* (Emphasis added.) Here, the evidence established that Dale was married to Janice, the victim's niece, and that all three resided together in the Simesters' home. Further the medical evidence established that the victim had no nutritional intake for at least one week, that his rigid fetal position took at least two weeks to develop and that his deep coma had to have existed for several days before his hospitalization. We find that these facts established that both Dale and Janice Simester should have reasonably known of the victim's condition long before the paramedics were summoned.

***

E. Critical Thinking

▶ The Child Abandonment statute requires that the actor have a special relationship to the child in question. Why do you think the Illinois legislature did not require such a relationship in the Endangering the life or health of a child statute?

▶ First offense Endangering the life or health of a child is a Class A misdemeanor. First offense Child Abandonment is a Class 4 felony. If you were a member of the Illinois General Assembly being interviewed by the media, how would you justify this difference in classification?

▶ Imagine you are a patrol officer with the City Police. You have stopped a vehicle driven by Max Crude on suspicion of Driving Under the Influence of Alcohol. A chemical analysis of Crude's breath indicates an alcohol concentration over twice the legal limit. Also in the vehicle at the time of the stop is Crude's son, Rex, and Rex's best friend, both of whom are ten years old. You cite Max for DUI. What other charge(s) will you consider filing?

▶ The statutes listed in this Chapter show that an omission may satisfy the *actus reus* requirement of certain crimes based upon a special relationship. Are there relationships in addition to that of a "parent to a child" or a "caregiver to the elderly or disabled" where you think the law should require one to take affirmative action where appropriate?

II. The Criminal Act of Possession

A. Comment

The voluntary act of possession may qualify as a violation of criminal law. This type of offense often involves the possession of narcotics, stolen property, or unlawful weapons.

Possession may be either actual or constructive. A person who has an item in his or her physical possession, in a pocket for example, is deemed to have the item in actual possession. If there is no evidence of actual possession, it may be determined that the person is in constructive possession of the item. Illinois courts have ruled that for a finding of constructive possession it must be shown not only that the defendant had knowledge of the presence of the item but that the defendant also had immediate and exclusive control of the area where the item was found. Consider the following cases in which constructive possession was at issue.

B. Cases

In the *Flores* case the appellate court considers the defendant's claim that the State failed to prove beyond a reasonable doubt that he was in possession of cannabis which had been seized from under the hood of his car.

In the *Feazell* case which follows, the defendant appealed his convictions contending the State had failed to prove he was in constructive possession of the drugs and weapons.

PEOPLE v. FLORES
231 Ill.App. 3d 813, 173 Ill.Dec. 325, 596 N.E.2d 1204, (4 Dist. 1992)

[Case citations omitted.]

Presiding Justice GREEN delivered the opinion of the court:

BACKGROUND

On March 26, 1991, the circuit court of McLean County entered judgment on a jury verdict finding defendant Eugenio Flores guilty of possession of more than 30 grams but less than 500 grams of cannabis, but not guilty of possession with the intent to deliver cannabis.

***

At trial State Trooper Layfield, the arresting officer, testified as follows: (1) on February 1, 1990, while on patrol with the "Valkyrie" team, a drug interdiction patrol, she initiated a traffic stop of a 1981 Oldsmobile automobile driven by defendant for speeding northbound on I-55; (2) there were two other male occupants in defendant's automobile; (3) when asked for a driver's license, defendant produced a Missouri traffic citation; (4) a State and national computer check indicated defendant's driver's license had been suspended in California; (5) the two men in defendant's automobile were illegal aliens and could not speak English; (6) defendant was placed under arrest and transported to the McLean County building; (7) she also transported the other two men to the McLean County building until the United States Immigration and Naturalization Service

(INS) could be notified; (8) defendant's automobile was towed by Jerry Brimmer's wrecker service because none of the occupants had a valid driver's license to drive the automobile, and defendant was unable to prove ownership; and (9) when defendant attempted to retake possession of the automobile on February 3, 1990, she arrested him for the present offense.***

In addition, Sergeant Shumaker, of the Illinois State Police, testified as follows: (1) he was working in the vehicle identification section when defendant's automobile had been towed to Brimmer's garage; (2) he was requested to "process" the automobile to determine ownership; (3) on February 2, 1990 (the morning after defendant's automobile was impounded), he went to Brimmer's garage; (4) when he got there the garage door was open, and Brimmer was sitting on steps nearby; (5) he first located the vehicle identification number in the left front window; (6) he then located the Federal sticker which also contained the vehicle identification number and is either attached to the left front door or left front door pillar; (7) after he checked those numbers, he released the hood latch from inside the automobile to check the body tag, which is located on the engine and which indicates the plant the automobile was produced at, the model and sometimes the production number; (8) as he raised the hood of the automobile, he observed a semi-clear plastic bag lying on the front wheel well on the left side of the automobile; and (9) he observed two containers wrapped in aluminum foil which contained stems, seeds, and plant material resembling cannabis.

Shumaker testified on cross-examination as follows: (1) at trial he identified fingerprint powder on the plastic bag he found in the left wheel well of the automobile; (2) their procedure is to check for fingerprints; (3) he did not wear rubber gloves when he picked up the plastic bag; (4) his fingerprints would probably be on the plastic bag; (5) the tinfoil was probably not checked for fingerprints; and (6) he ran a computer check through the State of California and on February 2, 1990, and July 1990, the license plates on defendant's automobile were registered to a Mr. Jesus Preciado in Escondido, California.

Jerry Brimmer testified, and essentially corroborated the testimony of Sergeant Shumaker regarding the search which led to finding the cannabis on the left front wheel well of defendant's automobile. In addition Brimmer testified as follows: (1) he towed defendant's automobile to his personal two-car garage because the police requested indoor storage; (2) no other automobile was located in the garage; (3) the garage was always locked, but he was not sure of whether the automobile was locked; (4) only he and his wife, Trooper Layfield, and Sergeant Shumaker had access to the garage; and (5) he was present when Trooper Layfield and Sergeant Shumaker searched the automobile.

***

Defendant was the principal witness for the defense and testified...he was surprised the police found the cannabis, and he never saw it there when he had previously checked the water and oil under the hood; and...he never uses drugs.

ANALYSIS

To establish possession of the cannabis by defendant, the State must prove two elements (1) defendant had knowledge of the presence of controlled substance; and (2) the controlled substance was in the defendant's "immediate and exclusive control." Possession can be either actual, requiring an act of physical dominion over the controlled substance, or constructive, which can be inferred if the defendant had exclusive control over the premises where the controlled substance was found. Knowledge of the location of the controlled substance alone does not prove possession. However, because of the difficulty in proving knowledge, when actual or constructive possession is established, generally the element of knowledge can be inferred from the surrounding facts and circumstances.

Defendant maintains that, here, possession cannot be inferred when the only evidence connecting him to the cannabis was that he owned the automobile in which it was found, especially when no fingerprint evidence was presented. In particular, defendant contends the State failed to prove he had "immediate and exclusive" control over the cannabis, or the automobile where the cannabis was found, because (1) no evidence was presented concerning whether the two men who occupied his automobile had knowledge of the cannabis; and (2) the automobile was beyond his control and custody and accessible by others for at least 18 hours before the cannabis was found.

***

[H]ere, an inference of exclusive control by defendant over the cannabis can be established because defendant owned the automobile, and more importantly, because the cannabis was found in an area of the automobile to which only the owner ordinarily has access. The evidence at trial established that defendant had owned the automobile for several months prior to the traffic stop and was driving at the time of the stop. Defendant testified that he personally checked the water and oil levels under the hood. The jury knew there were two passengers in defendant's automobile at the time of the traffic stop, and could reasonably have concluded that the passengers would not have had access to that area of defendant's automobile. In any event, the requirement that defendant have immediate and exclusive control over the controlled substance, or the premises where the controlled substance was found, does not rule out joint control.

Additionally, the jury was aware that the automobile was towed and out of defendant's immediate and exclusive control for approximately 18 hours. However, the evidence also established that during that time the automobile was in a locked garage, and the only individuals who had access to the automobile were Trooper Layfield, Sergeant Shumaker, Brimmer, and Brimmer's wife. The jury could reasonably have concluded that those individuals would not have placed the cannabis under the hood of defendant's automobile. Under the circumstances, the lack of fingerprint evidence would not necessarily raise a reasonable doubt. Once the jury concluded defendant was in constructive possession of the cannabis, defendant's knowledge of the presence of the cannabis could reasonably be inferred.***

CONCLUSION

In determining whether the evidence in a criminal case is sufficient to support a verdict of guilt, we view the evidence in a light most favorable to the prosecution and determine whether, under that evidence, a rational trier of fact could have found that each essential element of the offense was proved beyond a reasonable doubt. We find the proof met that test here.***

PEOPLE v. FEAZELL
248 Ill.App. 3d 538, 188 Ill.Dec. 1, 618 N.E.2d 571 (1 Dist.),
appeal denied, 152 Ill.2d 567, 190 Ill.Dec. 898, 622 N.E.2d 1215 (1993)

[Case citations omitted.]

Justice HOFFMAN delivered the opinion of the court:

BACKGROUND

After a jury trial, defendant, Wydell Feazell, was convicted of possession of a controlled substance with intent to deliver, possession of cannabis with intent to deliver, unlawful use of weapons, and unlawful use of weapons by a felon. Defendant now appeals and we consider... whether the evidence at trial was sufficient to prove beyond a reasonable doubt that defendant constructively possessed the drugs and weapons.

On June 1, 1988, defendant was arrested without a warrant after an altercation with his neighbor. Without a search warrant, the police searched the apartment where defendant was arrested and seized cocaine, cannabis, and weapons.

...Officer David Strain testified that on June 1, 1988, he responded to a complaint from defendant's neighbor who said that defendant attacked him with an ax handle and a gun. From a previous incident, Strain knew defendant lived at 320 West Evergreen.

Strain, accompanied by Sergeant Phillip Watzke and Officer David Schmidt, arrived at that address without an arrest or search warrant. Strain saw defendant and his son, Wydell Jr., in the yard. When defendant saw the officers, he ran up to the third-floor apartment in the building. The officers followed him but the door was locked with a combination lock. They knocked and shouted defendant's name but he did not answer. Strain testified that, without being asked, Wydell Jr. came up to the third floor, entered the combination, and unlocked the door. Defendant was arrested, handcuffed, and read his *Miranda* rights.

The officers recovered a bloody ax handle on the back porch. Strain testified that the officers were discussing obtaining a search warrant when defendant asked if that could be avoided because he thought the police would ransack the apartment while searching it. Strain explained to defendant that he could accompany the officers while they conducted a plain view search for the gun involved in the aggravated battery. Defendant agreed. From an open pantry shelf, Strain recovered bags of white powder and crushed green plant, which he suspected was cocaine and cannabis, and miscellaneous types of ammunition.

...In the search of the apartment, [Officer] Schmidt recovered an antique gun, two cross bows, a sawed-off rifle which defendant said was real, a machine gun, and an Uzi submachine gun. They did not, however, recover the gun allegedly used in the aggravated battery.***

Wydell Jr., defendant's 13-year-old son, referred to the third-floor apartment as defendant's house and stated that he lived with defendant there from "time to time."

***

[Officer] Strain...testified that when they recovered the cannabis, defendant told the police that it was his. Defendant also said that the rocky white powder was cocaine but the other bags were fake. Further, defendant told the police that the Uzi submachine gun was a replica but the shot gun was real.***

Defendant testified that at the time of his arrest, he lived at 1511 North Wieland. He admitted that he kept clothes in the third-floor apartment and he was there three to four times a week. He explained that several other people had the combination to the apartment for construction or business purposes. After he was arrested, the officers told him they would get a search warrant unless defendant told them they could search the apartment. Defendant admitted that he told the officers they could search. Defendant testified that he and [another individual] were the stockholders of a corporation that owned the apartment building. Defendant denied ever seeing the contraband that was seized from the apartment and denied that he told the police it was his. He recognized the rifle as belonging to a former tenant. Defendant told the officers that none of the seized items were his.***

ANALYSIS

To support a finding of constructive possession, the State must prove that the defendant knew the contraband was present and that it was in defendant's immediate and exclusive control. Knowledge may be proved by evidence of defendant's acts, declarations, or conduct from which it can be inferred that he knew the contraband existed in the place where it was found. Constructive possession may be proved by showing that defendant controlled the premises where the contraband was found.

The elements of possession or knowledge are questions of fact for the jury and are rarely susceptible to direct proof. The evidence at trial must be viewed in a light most favorable to the prosecution and the reviewing court should not substitute its judgment for the jury's when the evidence is conflicting.***

Viewing the evidence presented at trial in a light most favorable to the State, Strain testified that when they discovered the cannabis, defendant admitted it was his. He also demonstrated knowledge of the cocaine and the weapons when he told the officers which items were real. Also, Strain and Schmidt testified that defendant told them all of the seized items were his. Further, Strain knew defendant lived there from a previous incident and even defendant's son referred to the apartment as defendant's home. Even though other people testified they had access to the apartment, the jury may not have found that testimony credible. The evidence was sufficient to find that defendant had constructive possession of the drugs and weapons seized in the apartment.***

D. Critical Thinking

► In both the *Flores* and *Feazell* cases, the defendants were found to be in constructive possession of the evidence at trial despite testimony that others could have had access to the areas where the items were found. Imagine you were the prosecutor in each of these cases. In your closing argument how would you have addressed this issue?

► In both the *Flores* and *Feazell* cases, the defendants made statements to the police. As a juror, would you have had a reasonable doubt regarding constructive possession without the defendant's statements? What if the defendant's fingerprints had been located on the evidence?

► In both the *Flores* and *Feazell* cases, the defendants testified on their own behalf. Do you agree that the reviewing [appellate] court should not substitute its assessment of the credibility of the witnesses for that of the jury?

D. Questions

Please choose the correct answer for the following questions.

1. Generally, which of the following is required for a violation of a criminal law in Illinois?

a. *actus reus*
b. *mens rea*
c. concurrence of act and intent
d. all of the above

2. An omission may serve as which necessary component of a crime?

a. *actus reus*
b. *mens rea*
c. concurrence
d. none of the above

3. A duty to act may arise based upon which of the following?

a. statute
b. contract
c. relationship with the actor
d. all of the above

4. Which of the following is a material element of every criminal offense in Illinois?

a. a criminal thought
b. a moral obligation
c. a voluntary act
d. all of the above

5. The Illinois statute, Endangering the life or health of a child, may be committed by which of the following?

a. the parent of a child
b. the child's babysitter
c. a family friend
d. any of the above

CHAPTER FOUR

Criminal Liability

For most crimes in Illinois, the defendant's criminal intent, or *mens rea*, must be established along with the criminal act. *Mens rea* may be thought of as the "guilty mind." The general principle is that a voluntary act causing harm must be intended by the actor. While an insulting or provoking touch may suffice for a battery charge against the actor, bumping into another shopper at a crowded mall on December 24 will negate the element of criminal intent if the contact was accidental rather than intentional. In other words, criminal law requires intent on the part of the actor before punishment will be imposed.

I. The Actor's Mental State

A. Comments

Some criminal statutes in Illinois used to contain vague descriptions of the required mental state. Terms formerly used in defining statutes included: "rude and licentious," "officious," "evil intent," and "without due caution or circumspection." Others required no mental state. In some instances, courts held that if no mental state was mentioned, then none was required, making it an absolute liability offense. At times, courts found it necessary to imply a particular mental state when none was stated. Many of the statutes have since been revamped to utilize more standardized mental states.

B. Statute

720 ILCS 5/4-3 Mental state

(a) A person is not guilty of an offense, other than an offense which involves absolute liability, unless, with respect to each element described by the statute defining the offense, he acts while having one of the mental states described in Sections 4-4 through 4-7.

(b) If the statute defining an offense prescribed a particular mental state with respect to the offense as a whole, without distinguishing among the elements thereof, the prescribed mental state applies to each such element. If the statute does not prescribe a particular mental state applicable to an element of an offense (other than an offense which involves absolute liability), any mental state defined in Sections 4-4, 4-5 or 4-6 is applicable.

(c) Knowledge that certain conduct constitutes an offense, or knowledge of the existence, meaning, or application of the statute defining an offense, is not an element of the offense unless the statute clearly defines it as such.

C. Case

The following case demonstrates the analysis applied by the court when a defining statute does not include a mental state.

PEOPLE v. ABDUL-MUTAKABBIR
295 Ill.App.3d 558, 229 Ill.Dec. 767, 692 N.E.2d 756 (1 Dist. 1998)

[Case citations omitted.]

BACKGROUND

On November 22, 1993, by Illinois Supreme Court order, the defendant was suspended from the practice of law for a period of three years. On January 24, 1994, an attorney with the Attorney Registration and Disciplinary Commission (ARDC) sent a letter to the defendant stating that the ARDC had been informed that, although the defendant was suspended from the practice of law, he was still holding himself out as an attorney. The letter stated that the defendant was still listed as an attorney on the directory in the lobby of his office building and a recorded message on the defendant's business phone identified him as an attorney. The letter reminded the defendant of his duties as a disciplined attorney and requested that he comply with the applicable Supreme Court Rules.

On April 24, 1996, an eight-count misdemeanor complaint was filed charging the defendant with having "*knowingly* and falsely represented himself to be an attorney authorized to practice law." (Emphasis added.) A jury trial was held.

During the jury instruction conference, defense counsel requested that the word "knowledge" be inserted into the [jury] instructions for false personation of a judicial official. The State argued that the offense is an absolute liability offense and does not require a mental state. The trial judge agreed with the State and instructed the jury that to sustain the charge the State must prove beyond a reasonable doubt that "the defendant falsely represented himself to be an attorney authorized to practice law."

The jury found the defendant guilty of all eight counts as charged.*** The defendant now appeals, contending that the trial court erred when it refused to instruct the jury that knowledge was an element of the offense of false personation of a judicial official.

ANALYSIS

The first step in our analysis requires us to determine what, if any, mental state is necessary for a violation of section 32-5 of the Code.

Section 32-5 provides in pertinent part that "[a] person who falsely represents himself to be an attorney authorized to practice law *** commits a Class B misdemeanor." Although the statute does not contain express language describing a mental state as an element of the offense, it is not, as the State contends, an absolute liability offense.***

Given our conclusion that section 32-5 is not an absolute liability offense, we must next determine which mental state applies to "each element described by the statute defining the offense." When, as in this case, a statute neither prescribes a particular mental state nor creates an absolute liability offense, then the mental state applicable to each element is either intent, knowledge, or recklessness.

The defendant argues, and we agree, that knowledge is the appropriate mental state applicable to the falsity element of the offense set forth in section 32-5 of the Code. To state that a person commits an offense by falsely representing a fact to be true without requiring that the person know of the falsity of the representation is the equivalent of absolute liability. Consequently, we hold that in order to convict an individual of an offense under section 32-5 of the Code for falsely representing himself to be an attorney authorized to practice law, the State is required to prove beyond a reasonable doubt that such a person knew that his representation was false when made.

CONCLUSION

…In cases where a person is charged with falsely representing himself to be an attorney authorized to practice law, there will rarely be a question as to whether the representation was false, but there may well be a question as to whether the person knew that the representation was false, especially in the case of a recently suspended attorney. Accordingly, the trial court erred in refusing the defendant's request that the word "knowledge" be inserted into the [jury] instruction setting forth the elements of the offense charged in this case.***

D. Comments

The appellate court determined that the misdemeanor offense of falsely representing one's self to be an attorney authorized to practice law is not an absolute liability offense. Consequently, the defendant must have acted "knowingly" at the time the offenses were committed. The court ruled that some criminal offenses require a particular mental state on the part of the actor even though it is not specifically mentioned in the defining statute. The requisite mental state may be implied. If a criminal statute does not state the particular mental state required, then the mental state applicable to each element of the offense is either intent, knowledge, or recklessness.

II. Levels of *Mens Rea*

A. Comments

In an attempt to simplify the description of mental states in the laws defining criminal offenses, the Illinois Code now defines the commonly used terms "with intent" and "knowingly or with knowledge," as well as the non-intent terms "recklessly" and "negligently." Note the definitions of these mental states in the statutes which follow.

B. Statutes

720 ILCS 5/4-4 Intent

A person intends, or acts intentionally or with intent, to accomplish a result or engage in conduct described by the statute defining the offense, when his conscious objective or purpose is to accomplish that result or engage in that conduct.

720 ILCS 5/4-5 Knowledge

A person knows, or acts knowingly or with knowledge of:

(a) The nature of attendant circumstances of his conduct, described by the statute defining the offense, when he is consciously aware that his conduct is of such nature or that such circumstances exist. Knowledge of a material fact includes awareness of the substantial probability that such fact exists.

(b) The result of his conduct, described by the statute defining the offense, when he is consciously aware that such result is practically certain to be caused by his conduct.

Conduct performed knowingly or with knowledge is performed willfully, within the meaning of a statute using the latter term, unless the statute clearly requires another meaning.

720 ILCS 5/4-6 Recklessness

A person is reckless or acts recklessly, when he consciously disregards a substantial and unjustifiable risk that circumstances exist or that a result will follow, described by the statute defining the offense; and such disregard constitutes a gross deviation from the standard of care which a reasonable person would exercise in the situation. An act performed recklessly is performed wantonly, within the meaning of a statute using the latter term, unless the statute clearly requires another meaning.

720 ILCS 5/4-7 Negligence

A person is negligent, or acts negligently, when he fails to be aware of a substantial and unjustifiable risk that circumstances exist or a result will follow, described by the statute defining the offense; and such failure constitutes a substantial deviation from the standard of care which a reasonable person would exercise in the situation.

C. Case

The defendant was convicted of involuntary manslaughter for the death of her three-month-old son, who died of heat stroke after she left him unattended in her car for several hours. She contends that the evidence at trial failed to prove she acted recklessly.

PEOPLE v. KOLZOW
301 Ill.App.3d 1, 234 Ill.Dec. 563, 703 N.E.2d 424 (1 Dist. 1998),
appeal denied, 182 Ill.2d 561, 236 Ill.Dec. 672, 707 N.E.2d 1242 (1999).

[Case citations omitted.]

JUSTICE O'MARA FROSSARD delivered the opinion of the court:

BACKGROUND

Defendant, Donna Kolzow, related the following in her statements to police: on the night of August 11, 1996, defendant was out with her three-month-old baby, Jeffrey. From 11 p.m. until 2 a.m., she and the child were driving around in a car with a friend of defendant, Eileen Hoover. While driving around, defendant called Officer Jeffrey Simpson, an on-duty Riverside police officer, whom she and Hoover later met at a parking lot around 1 a.m. After feeding the child with a bottle at approximately 2 a.m., she drove Hoover home. In her initial statement to police, defendant said that she and the baby spent the night at Hoover's home until she drove home at 6:30 a.m. However, in a subsequent statement, defendant said that after she dropped Hoover off at home, she ran into Officer Simpson again, who asked her to meet him at the Riverside Swim Club. She met him, got out of her car to talk and drove home around 4:30 a.m. She and the baby arrived home around 5 a.m., but instead of going inside, defendant parked her car in a nearby parking lot and read a book. She stated that she did not go inside because she did not want to wake her sleeping stepmother. At 6:30 a.m., defendant said she noticed her stepmother's car was gone and parked her car in front of the house. She turned off the engine, closed the driver's window, and locked the car. Leaving the baby in the car, defendant then went in the house. She stated she immediately went to the bathroom as she had diarrhea. Defendant said she then set the alarm for 9:30 a.m., lay on the couch and fell asleep. She said she forgot about the baby, who was locked outside in the car.

Defendant stated the alarm never went off and that she awoke at 10:30 a.m. on her own. She said she remembered the baby was still in the car when she noticed he was not in the playpen. She went out to the car and saw the child's face was completely purple. After bringing him into the house, she said she felt his hands and knew he was dead. She then called her father and her workplace. When her sister called the house, defendant told her the baby was dead.

Officer James Glosniak of the Hillside Police Department arrived at the scene shortly after 11 a.m. on August 12, 1996, in response to a call from one of the defendant's relatives. He testified that, when he arrived, the rear windows of the car were down about four inches and the front windows were closed. He said the car was facing west. The child was inside the house, and the officer found no pulse. The child's body was still warm, and his cheeks and hands were a dark, reddish purple color. Defendant told the officer that she had left the baby in the car from 7 a.m. until 10:30 a.m. that morning with the windows rolled up. However, when later asked whether she had rolled the windows down, she stated she had not touched anything in the car since she removed the baby. Realizing that the child could not be resuscitated, Officer Glosniak called his supervisor to the scene.

An autopsy conducted the next day revealed the baby died of heat stroke, and Dr. Edmond Donoghue of the Cook County Medical Examiner's office concluded that "parental neglect [was] a significant factor" in the child's death. Donoghue noted that the baby's nutrition, hydration and cleanliness were good and stated on cross-examination that it appeared the child had been well cared for.***

ANALYSIS

Under the Illinois Criminal Code of 1961, a person commits involuntary manslaughter when he or she "unintentionally kills an individual without lawful justification***[and] his [or her] acts whether lawful or unlawful which cause the death are such as are likely to cause death or great bodily harm to some individual, and he [or she] performs them recklessly...."

Defendant asserts that in the present case, there was no evidence she knew the car would become so overheated that it was a danger to her baby and thus there was no evidence she consciously disregarded any risk. Therefore, she argues, there was insufficient proof of recklessness. We disagree, and find the record contains sufficient evidence to support a conviction for involuntary manslaughter; specifically, that defendant left her three-month-old son in the vehicle, consciously disregarding a substantial and unjustifiable risk of death or great bodily harm to her son.

We find that a rational trier of fact could certainly interpret the evidence presented, including the statement of defendant herself, as supporting the conclusion that defendant acted recklessly in leaving her baby unattended in the car. The evidence in the record supports the State's theory, and the trial court's conclusion, that defendant left the child unattended in an effort to get some uninterrupted sleep. First, defendant claimed to have set her alarm before she lay down to go to sleep, supporting the inference she purposely intended to nap rather than just fall asleep. In addition, she waited outside her stepmother's home from 5 a.m. to 6:30 a.m. even though she had been up all night, thereby avoiding any possibility that her decision to leave the child unattended would be questioned by the stepmother. Also, before defendant went into the house, leaving the baby in the car, she locked the car and closed the windows, further supporting the conclusion that she did not plan to come immediately back out to retrieve the child after going to the bathroom. Finally, the car was found with each back window opened about four inches, which indicates defendant was planning to leave the child in the car and knew it could become hot.***

Defendant also asserts that, because she was a new mother, she was unaware of the danger of leaving the child unattended in the car, and she argues there was no indication she knew how high the temperature in the car could get. However, defendant was not charged with murder for intentionally killing her child; she was charged with involuntary manslaughter, which requires a mental state of recklessness. In general, a defendant acts recklessly when he or she is aware that his conduct might result in death or great bodily harm, although that result is not substantially certain to occur. We believe a reasonable person would be aware of the risks in leaving a three-month-old infant unattended in a parked car for four hours on a summer day, and find the evidence supports the trial court's finding that defendant acted recklessly by consciously disregarding that clear and obvious risk.

In the present case, the evidence was sufficient to support a conviction for involuntary manslaughter.***

D. Comments

In the above case, the charged offense of involuntary manslaughter specifically provided the required mental state. The Court of Appeals reviewed the facts to determine whether the defendant acted recklessly as defined in 720 ILCS 5/4-6. In its opinion, the court explains how it reached the conclusion that defendant did, in fact, meet the required mental state to uphold the conviction.

III. Absolute Liability

A. Comments

Strict liability offenses are crimes for which no mental state, or *mens rea*, is required. For example, an individual stopped by police for driving ten miles over the posted speed limit cannot avoid a citation simply by stating they did not intend to speed. In Illinois offenses for which the actor may be held strictly liable are known as "absolute liability" offenses. The following statute describes the type of offense for which an individual may be held criminally liable without possessing a particular mental state at the time the offense is committed.

B. Statute

720 ILCS 5/4-9 Absolute liability

A person may be guilty of an offense without having, as to each element thereof, one of the mental states described in Sections 4-4 through 4-7 if the offense is a misdemeanor which is not punishable by incarceration or by a fine exceeding $500, or the statute defining the offense clearly indicates a legislative purpose to impose absolute liability for the conduct described.

C. Case

This case provides an example of how Illinois courts determine whether a statute which contains no required mental state is in fact an absolute liability offense. In this case, the defendant was driving a borrowed car that was uninsured.

PEOPLE v. O'BRIEN
197 Ill.2d 88, 257 Ill.Dec. 669, 754 N.E.2d 327 (2001)

[Case citations omitted.]

Justice THOMAS delivered the opinion of the court:

The issue presented in this appeal is whether section 3-707 of the Illinois Vehicle Code (623 ILCS 5/3-707), which prohibits the operation of an uninsured motor vehicle, is an absolute liability offense. We hold that it is.

BACKGROUND

Defendant, Lewis O'Brien, was charged by traffic citation with violating section 3-707 of the Illinois Vehicle Code (the Code). Section 3-707 provides, in relevant part:

> "No person shall operate a motor vehicle unless the motor vehicle is covered by a liability insurance policy in accordance with Section 7-601 of this Code.
> Any person who fails to comply with a request by a law enforcement officer for display of evidence of insurance, as required under Section 7-602 of this Code, shall be deemed to be operating an uninsured motor vehicle.

Any operator of a motor vehicle subject to registration under this Code who is convicted of violating this Section is guilty of a business offense and shall be required to pay a fine in excess of $500, but not more than $1,000. However, no person charged with violating this Section shall be convicted if such person produces in court satisfactory evidence that at the time of the arrest the motor vehicle was covered by a liability insurance policy in accordance with Section 7-601 of this Code."

The sole witness at defendant's bench trial was Officer Stephen Mechling of the University of Illinois Police Department. Officer Mechling testified that, on June 10, 1999, he stopped defendant's vehicle because the license plate registration sticker on that vehicle had expired. Defendant explained that he had borrowed the car and therefore did not know that the sticker had expired. Officer Mechling then asked defendant whether the vehicle was insured, and defendant stated that he did not know. When defendant was unable to produce proof that the car was insured, Officer Mechling issued defendant a citation for operating an uninsured motor vehicle.

Defendant moved for a directed verdict. In that motion, defendant conceded that, if section 3-707 is an absolute liability offense, the State had established a *prima facie* case. Defendant argued, however, that section 3-707 is *not* an absolute liability offense but instead requires proof of a culpable mental state. According to defendant, because the State failed to prove that defendant either knew, or should have known, that the borrowed vehicle was uninsured, the State failed to prove defendant guilty of violating section 3-707. The trial court denied defendant's motion, holding that section 3-707 is an absolute liability offense. When no additional evidence was presented, the trial court found defendant guilty and imposed a fine of $501 plus court costs.

Defendant appealed, and the appellate court reversed his conviction. In doing so, the appellate court held that neither the plain language of nor the public policy underlying section 3-707 justifies the imposition of absolute liability. We allowed the State's petition for leave to appeal.

ANALYSIS

The issue in this case is whether section 3-707 creates an absolute liability offense. When construing a statute, this court's primary objective is to ascertain and give effect to the legislature's intent. We begin with the language of the statute, which must be given its plain and ordinary meaning.***

The legislature's clear intent to impose absolute liability can be gleaned from several sources. First, and most importantly, the plain language of section 3-707 unquestionably provides for absolute liability. Indeed, the language could not be clearer: "*No person shall operate* a motor vehicle unless the motor vehicle is covered by a liability insurance policy in accordance with Section 7-601 of this Code" (emphasis added). Section 7-601, in turn, provides that "*[n]o person shall operate****a motor vehicle designed to be used on a public highway unless the motor vehicle is covered by a

46

liability insurance policy." (Emphasis added.) Neither statute makes any exception for any class of operators, and both statutes employ the word "shall," which this court has construed as a clear expression of legislative intent to impose a mandatory obligation.*** Second, the relatively minor penalty that attaches to a violation of section 3-707 weighs heavily in favor of a legislative purpose to impose absolute liability.***

In this case, defendant was never facing either great punishment or "a long term of imprisonment." On the contrary, the crime established by section 3-707 is a "business offense," which by definition is not punishable by incarceration. Moreover, the penalty for violating section 3-707 (a $501 to $1,000 fine) only slightly exceeds the $500 statutory maximum for *per se* absolute liability offenses.***

...[W]e find that chapter 3, article VII, of the Code is replete with penal statutes containing a culpable mental state...Section 3-701(1) provides that "no person shall operate, nor shall an owner *knowingly* permit to be operated" a vehicle that lacks proper evidence of registration. (Emphasis added.) Likewise, section 3-702(a)(1) provides that "[n]o person shall operate, nor shall an owner *knowingly* permit to be operated" a vehicle for which the registration has been cancelled, suspended, or revoked. (Emphasis added.) Section 3-702(b) provides that "[n]o person shall use, nor shall any owner use or *knowingly* permit the use of" any vehicle registration that has been cancelled, suspended, or revoked. (Emphasis added.) Section 3-703 provides that "[n]o person shall ***knowingly permit the use of any [evidence of vehicle registration] by one not entitled thereto." (Emphasis added.) Finally, section 3-710 provides that "[n]o person shall display evidence of insurance to a law enforcement officer, court, or officer of the court, *knowing* there is no valid insurance in effect on the motor vehicle." (Emphasis added.)

CONCLUSION

In sum, we hold that, both on its face and in the context of related provisions of the Code, the plain language of section 3-707 clearly indicates a legislative purpose to impose absolute liability. We therefore reverse the judgment of the appellate court and affirm the judgment of the circuit court.***

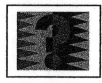

D. Questions

Please choose the correct answer for the following questions.

1. If an Illinois statute does not include a mental state, then:

a. none is required
b. a mental state may be implied
c. the defendant must have acted "knowingly"
d. none of the above

2. Today, mental states commonly listed in Illinois statutes include:

a. rude & licentious
b. officious
c. with due caution & circumspection
d. none of the above

3. A person whose conscious objective or purpose is to accomplish a particular result or engage in certain conduct, acts:

a. with intent
b. with knowledge
c. recklessly
d. negligently

4. A person acts negligently when:

a. she is consciously aware that such result is practically certain to be caused by her conduct
b. she intends to accomplish a certain result
c. her conduct is performed willfully
d. none of the above

5. Generally, an absolute liability offense is:

a. only for exceeding the speed limit
b. any misdemeanor offense
c. a misdemeanor not punishable by incarceration
d. a felony offense

CHAPTER FIVE

Parties to Crime
And the Accountability Theory

The person who acts as a lookout for a burglar, the person who hold the victim while another strikes him, the person who drives the car so his passenger can shoot a pedestrian. What do they all have in common? They may all be held criminally liable for the substantive offense under the Illinois accountability theory.

Under common law, the person who actually committed the crime was known as the principal in the first degree. Anyone who aided and abetted, in other words, was present and assisted in the commission of the crime, was a principal in the second degree. An aider and abettor not present at the time the crime was committed was known as an accessory before the fact. An individual who harbored or protected the criminal was deemed an accessory after the fact.

The common law classifications of parties to a crime are no longer recognized in Illinois. Prior Illinois statutes modified the common law distinctions between principal in the first degree, the second degree, and accessories before the fact. Those who would have been principals in the second degree, or accessories before the fact under common law, were principals in the first degree. Sound confusing? The current statute follows the approach of the former law, but provides a much clearer statement of the law regarding parties to crime.

I. Accountability

A. Comments

In Illinois, parties to a crime may be prosecuted under a theory of accountability. Accountability is not a crime by itself, but rather is a method by which an individual may be held criminally liable for an offense committed by another. Under accountability principles, the defendant will be charged and tried for the substantive offense. The accountability theory is not the same as guilt by association. The defendant's guilt is established through behavior. The State must prove that the defendant solicited, aided, abetted, agreed, or attempted to aid another person in the planning or the commission of the offense. In deciding whether accountability has been established, the trier of fact may consider such factors as defendant's presence at the scene of the crime; his failure to disassociate himself from the crime; as well as continued association with the perpetrator after the criminal act; flight from the scene; failure to report the incident; acceptance of proceeds from the crime; and concealment or destruction of evidence. The State must also establish that the defendant had the mental state to facilitate or promote commission of the offense. Unless the accomplice *intends* to aid the commission of a crime, no guilt will attach. However, should the State establish the accomplice's intent to aid in *a* crime, the accomplice will be held criminally liable for all criminal acts done in accomplishing the intended crime.

The accountability statute addresses the various situations which may arise. Note that Subsection 5-2(b) of the statute below indicates there may be situations in which an individual may be held legally accountable under circumstances not included in the accountability statute, but stated in a different statute. In that case, the particular statute under which the defendant is prosecuted prevails. An example of such a statute might be one imposing vicarious criminal liability on a tavern owner for the act of an employee who sells liquor to a minor.

Subsection 5-2(c) includes those situations that, at common law, involved the actions attributed to principals in the second degree and accessories before the fact. It is a comprehensive statement of liability based on actions such as counseling, aiding and abetting, or attempting to aid. To establish liability under this subsection, the State must establish the defendant possessed an "intent to promote or facilitate...commission" of the substantive offense. A conspiracy between the actor and the defendant may satisfy the requirements of this subsection.

Subsections (c)(1), (2) and (3) provide relief from accountability for the conduct of another under certain circumstances. Subsection (c)(1) provides that the "victim" of the criminal act does not share the guilt of the actor unless the particular statute so states. This is the case even if the person was a "willing" victim and counseled commission of the offense. An example would be a victim who pays money to his blackmailer. Even though the victim aided in the commission of the crime, the victim is not held criminally liable for the blackmail offense.

A defendant may also be found guilty under an accountability theory even though the identity of the principal is unknown. While the cases in this Chapter involve felony offenses, keep in mind that the following statutes apply to misdemeanors as well.

B. Statutes

720 ILCS 5/5-1 Accountability for conduct of another

A person is responsible for conduct which is an element of an offense if the conduct is either that of the person himself, or that of another and he is legally accountable for such conduct as provided in Section 5-2 [720 ILCS 5/5-2], or both.

720 ILCS 5/5-2 When accountability exists

A person is legally accountable for the conduct of another when:

(a) Having a mental state described by the statute defining the offense, he causes another to perform the conduct, and the other person in fact or by reason of legal incapacity lacks such a mental state; or

(b) The statute defining the offense makes him so accountable; or

(c) Either before or during the commission of an offense, and with the intent to promote or facilitate such commission, he solicits, aids, abets, agrees or attempts to aid, such other person in the planning or commission of the offense. However, a person is not so accountable, unless the statute defining the offense provides otherwise, if:

(1) He is a victim of the offense committed; or

(2) The offense is so defined that his conduct was inevitably incident to its commission; or

(3) Before the commission of the offense, he terminates his effort to promote or facilitate such commission, and does one of the following: wholly deprives his prior efforts of effectiveness in such commission, or gives timely warning to the proper law enforcement authorities, or otherwise makes proper effort to prevent the commission of the offense.

C. Case

In the following case, the evidence established that the victim, Rodney Collins, was shot by a member of defendant's gang. Although the defendant was not present at the scene of the crime, he was charged with Collins' murder on a theory of accountability. Note the defendant's role within the gang. The court held the defendant knew that when a fellow gang member took his gun to "take care of business" it meant there was going to be retribution for an earlier event. By supplying the gun, the defendant was found to have aided or attempted to aid in the commission of the subsequent shooting.

PEOPLE v. WARD
302 Ill.App.3d 550, 236 Ill.Dec. 285, 707 N.E.2d 130 (1 Dist. 1998),
appeal denied, 183 Ill.2d 593, 238 Ill.Dec. 719, 712 N.E.2d 823 (1999)

[Case citations omitted.]

Presiding Justice CAHILL delivered the opinion of the court:
BACKGROUND

On March 29, 1994, at about 5 p.m., 10-year-old Rodney Collins was with friends, riding his bicycle outside his home on Winchester Street in Chicago, Illinois. On the corner of 51st and Wentworth, two men made "pitchfork" hand signals, signifying allegiance to the Gangster Disciples street gang. The same men were also "throwing down the [five]," signifying disrespect for the Blackstones street gang. The Gangster Disciples is a gang affiliated with a larger group called the "Folks," and the Blackstones are affiliated with a group called the "People." The two groups are enemies. A few minutes after making the gang signals, the two men ran down Winchester and shouted, "[W]e got you hooks now." The two men began shooting at 10 to 15 children playing on the street. Two different kinds of gunfire were heard by witnesses. Rodney Collins was shot in the back. He later died from his injuries.

One of the detectives who investigated the shooting testified at trial that the defendant gave the following oral statement. Defendant was a Gangster Disciple and he was "working security" for a drug operation on 51st and Honore Streets on March 29, 1994. He was armed with a 9 millimeter handgun. Carl Brannigan, who was "chief of security" for the Gangster Disciples, and Michael Taylor approached him. Brannigan said "they were going to shoot the Blackstones on Winchester" and asked defendant for his weapon. Defendant handed Brannigan the gun, and Brannigan told defendant to "shut down the narcotics sales" for about three hours. Defendant then went to a house at 50th and Wolcott Streets and sat on the porch. A few moments later he heard more than 10 shots fired.

After a bench trial, defendant Antoine Ward was found guilty of Collins' murder and was sentenced to 29 years in prison. Defendant argues on appeal that the trial court erred, *inter alia*, in finding him guilty beyond a reasonable doubt. We affirm.

ANALYSIS

Defendant argues that there was no evidence that Brannigan participated in the shooting or that the gun he gave Brannigan was used to shoot Rodney Collins.***

To convict defendant on a theory of accountability, the State must prove: (1) defendant solicited, ordered, abetted, agreed, or attempted to aid another in the planning or commission of the crime; (2) defendant's participation took place before or during the commission of the crime; and (3) defendant had the concurrent intent to promote or facilitate the commission of the crime.***

The State was not required to prove that Brannigan was one of the shooters or that the shot that killed Collins came from the gun defendant gave to Brannigan. An armed, active member of a street gang in charge of security on a drug corner can fairly be described as one voluntarily attached to a group bent on illegal acts. The common criminal plan or purpose of the Gangster Disciples has decades of bloodshed as part of its history. That they were about such business in this case and that Ward attached himself to it is supported by the evidence before us. To suggest that so-called "security officers" can shield themselves from culpability by handing over weapons to other gang members and leaving the scene would be to mock the accountability statute.

CONCLUSION

Michael Taylor was present when Brannigan asked for the gun so "they" could "take care of business," and Michael Taylor was identified as a shooter in the murder that occurred shortly after. Defendant knew that "taking care of business" meant they were going to shoot Blackstones in retribution for an earlier incident and that the shooting was going to occur that day. We believe a reasonable trier of fact could infer from these facts that the gun was used, or that defendant intended that the gun be used, in the shooting and that defendant in doing so abetted or attempted to aid in the commission of the offense by supplying the gun.***

D. Critical Thinking

►Do you believe the court appropriately considered the defendant's role as "security officer" within the gang as a factor in determining whether he abetted or attempted to aid the shooting?

►The State was not required to prove that the shot that killed the Collins boy came from the gun defendant gave to his fellow gang member. How can defendant be convicted for that murder?

II. Aiding and Abetting

A. Comments

Under Illinois law, it is well established that one may aid and abet a principal without actively participating in the overt act itself. The defendant's intent to provide aid may be inferred from the character of his acts as well as the circumstances surrounding commission of the offense. While mere presence at the crime scene is not sufficient to create liability, there are several factors which the court may consider in determining a person has aided in the commission of a crime. The case in this section provides an example of the analysis the court will conduct in making this determination.

Should a defendant change his mind about giving aid to a principal, he may relieve himself of liability for the substantive crime by taking certain actions. Subsection (c)(3) of the accountability statute may be the answer for such an individual. This subsection exists to provide incentive to the defendant to stop his efforts, report the crime to law enforcement, and perhaps prevent the crime from occurring.

B. Case

In this case, the defendant was found guilty of the murder of Shelvin Johnson under an accountability theory. Defendant appeals his conviction alleging that accountability may not be shown by his mere presence at the scene of the crime, nor by a showing that defendant knew the crime was being committed. While that is true, the court points out other factors which raise the inference that the defendant aided in the commission of this crime.

PEOPLE v. HOUSTON
258 Ill.App.3d 364, 196 Ill.Dec. 229, 629 N.E.2d 774 (4 Dist. 1994)

[Case citations omitted]

Justice KNECHT delivered the opinion of the court:

BACKGROUND

Shelvin Johnson and Martinez Gill were partners in a cocaine-selling operation. In April 1992, they had a falling out. On May 10, 1992, Johnson and Jimmie "Junior" Ross went to Gill's mobile home. Thomas Houston spotted Ross outside the mobile home and asked what he was doing there. Ross responded that he hoped to buy drugs. After Houston left, Johnson and Ross broke into Gill's mobile home and stole a television set, a camera, drugs, and some cash.

At approximately midnight, Houston and Willie "Prince" McClain went to the mobile home of Willie Dorsey, Johnson's uncle. Houston and McClain were looking for Johnson. Dorsey informed them Johnson was at the Green Apartments.

At approximately 2 a.m. on May 11, 1992, McClain met up with Sara Ellen Beatty Lambert. Lambert asked McClain whether he could get her some cocaine; McClain stated she would have to wait because he had to "find somebody." McClain instructed Lambert to drive him around Champaign in her car, which she did. McClain later explained Gill's trailer had been broken into and McClain was searching for the culprit. Lambert picked up Gill and Houston. The group stopped at the Green Apartments approximately three times. On one occasion, McClain left the car and the sound of breaking glass could be heard. Upon returning to Lambert's car, McClain explained he had smashed the windows of Johnson's car.

At approximately 3:30 or 3:45 a.m., one of the passengers instructed Lambert to follow a tan Chevette. There were three passengers in the car, later identified as Johnson, Ross and Eunice Gwendolyn Penerman. As Lambert's car approached it, the Chevette came to a stop and a woman, later identified as Juvions "Michelle" Meeks Cooley Gillespie, approached the Chevette and began speaking with one of the passengers.

54

Lambert stopped her car next to the Chevette. She heard McClain say "give me the gun. Let me do it." Lambert believed McClain directed this request to Houston, but later acknowledged she was not certain. McClain, Gill and Houston all exited Lambert's car and approached the Chevette. Lambert saw both McClain and Gill fire the gun. Lambert heard Houston yell "something about somebody was running toward the field or toward the alley." She additionally testified "when the shooting was going on, I could hear talking and it seemed like they were worried about who was getting away, whether they thought they had not got somebody."

According to Lambert, after shots had been fired, Gill, McClain and Houston got back into her car. McClain fired a final shot into the Chevette. The men instructed Lambert to drive away. As she drove they requested her to increase her speed and disrespect stop signs. Lambert drove to the apartment of McClain's girlfriend. At the apartment, McClain gave Houston the murder weapon and instructed him to hide it. Houston took the gun and disappeared around the corner of the building. After instructing Lambert not to tell anyone what had happened, McClain permitted her to go home.

Johnson and Penerman died as a result of the bullet wounds. Ross and Gillespie were treated and recovered. Several days after the shootings, Lambert turned herself in to the police and reported McClain, Gill and Houston had been involved in the shootings. ***

A jury found defendant guilty of five counts of first degree murder as to Johnson, not guilty of the five counts of first degree murder of Penerman.... The trial court entered a conviction on each of the five counts of first degree murder of Johnson.

On appeal, defendant alleged he was improperly found guilty of the murder of Johnson under an accountability theory. ***

ANALYSIS

An individual is legally accountable for the actions of another when "[e]ither before or during the commission of an offense, and with the intent to promote or facilitate such commission, he solicits, aids, abets, agrees or attempts to aid, such other person in the planning or commission of the offense." As defendant correctly notes, accountability may not be established by his mere presence at the scene of a crime; nor may it be established by proof defendant had knowledge the crime was being committed. Rather, accountability must be established by a showing defendant (1) solicited, aided, abetted, agreed, or attempted the offense; (2) such participation in the offense took place before or during the offense; and (3) the defendant's participation was accompanied by a concurrent, specific intent to promote or facilitate the commission of the offense.

There was sufficient evidence from which the jury could have concluded Houston aided and abetted the murder of Johnson. Although mere presence at the scene of the crime does not render an accused accountable, if the evidence shows the accused was present at the crime without disapproving or opposing it, the trier of fact may *infer* he assented to the commission of the crime and thereby aided and abetted it. In addition to the accused's presence at the scene of the crime, without disassociating himself from the crime, other factors which raise inferences the accused aided in the commission of the crime include flight from the scene; continued association with the perpetrator after the criminal act; failure to report the incident; acceptance of illegal proceeds of the crime; and concealment or destruction of the evidence.

***

...Houston's conduct extended far beyond mere presence at the scene of the crime. After implicating Johnson and Ross in the theft of Gill's property, Houston accompanied Gill on a search for Johnson and Ross. He remained with them after McClain smashed the windows of Johnson's car. After hearing McClain say "give me the gun. Let me do it," Houston accompanied McClain and Gill to Johnson's car. No evidence was introduced indicating Houston attempted to prevent Gill and McClain from shooting Johnson and his companions. On the contrary, Houston alerted the gunmen one of Johnson's companions was attempting to escape. After the shots were fired, Houston fled the scene with Gill and McClain. He remained in their company, going to the apartment of McClain's girlfriend. After being given the murder weapon by McClain, Houston concealed it. Based upon this evidence, the jury could have reasonably inferred Houston aided and abetted the murder of Johnson.

The second element of accomplice liability was also proved. Houston's participation in the offense clearly took place both before and during the offense.

Finally, there was adequate evidence from which the jury could have concluded the State proved the third element of accomplice liability, that the defendant's participation was accompanied by a concurrent, specific intent to promote or facilitate the commission of the crime. Specific intent need not be shown by words of agreement. The jury may infer an agreement from the conduct of the accused in attaching himself to a group which combines to act in circumstances showing a common design to do an unlawful act to which all assent. Nor is it necessary for the State to prove the accused had the specific intent to promote or facilitate the crime with which he is charged. The law on accountability incorporates the common design rule, which provides that where two or more persons engage in a common criminal design, any acts in furtherance thereof committed by one party are considered to be the acts of all parties to the common design and all are accountable for those acts.

Thus, the State need only prove the accused had the specific intent to promote or facilitate *a* crime. Once the State proves the accused intended to promote or facilitate *a* crime, it has established the accused's responsibility for *any* criminal act done in furtherance of the intended crime.

Where the accused intended to promote or facilitate a battery, he may be held responsible for the death of the victim. With respect to the activity which results in the death of another, our supreme court has stated:

"Where one attaches himself to a group bent on illegal acts which are dangerous or homicidal in character, or which will probably or necessarily require the use of force and violence that could result in the taking of life unlawfully, he becomes criminally liable for any wrongdoings committed by other members of the group...even though he did not actively participate in the overt act itself."

Even if Houston did not intend for Johnson to be murdered, he is guilty of murder if he, along with Gill and McClain, formed a common plan to engage in an attack and Johnson was killed during the commission of that attack.***

CONCLUSION

In this case, Houston attached himself to Gill and McClain, who were involved in a search for the men who had stolen Gill's property. The jury could have inferred from the fact that Houston remained with them even after they smashed Johnson's car windows and especially after they brandished a gun and McClain stated "let me do it" when confronting Johnson, that Houston formed the intent to promote or facilitate an attack on Johnson. Houston's conduct after the shootings merely reinforces the inference he was a part of the group intent upon attacking the victims. For the foregoing reasons, Houston's conviction of first degree murder is affirmed.

C. Critical Thinking

► What could the defendant have done to avoid being held liable for murder?

► At what point did it become too late for the defendant to withdraw from the crime?

III. Common Design

A. Comments

Under the theories of accountability and the common design rule, Illinois law holds all parties to a common criminal design or agreement equally responsible for the consequences of those acts committed by any one of the group in furtherance of the common agreement. The common design rule requires the evidence show a design to incite or in some manner aid or assist in the crime. The law does not require each individual take an active part in the commission of the crime. Defendant may be guilty of an offense even though the defendant's intent may be to aid the principal in only one offense and he does not have the intent to commit other crimes that are in fact committed by the principal. For example, the driver of a get-away car may be found accountable for a murder committed during a bank robbery.

Proof of acts in furtherance of a common design to commit a crime need not be supported by words of agreement. As long as circumstances show a common design to do the unlawful act, to which all agree, then whatever is done in furtherance of the original design is considered the act of all. A common design may be inferred from the circumstances surrounding the unlawful conduct.

Although the defendant involved in a common design may be found guilty of the substantive offense, the court may, when imposing sentence, take into consideration defendant's lesser participation.

B. Case

The defendant's acts in the following case were particularly heinous. Defendant was held accountable for the murders of a mother and one of her children. The evidence indicated the defendant aided and abetted two co-perpetrators in the planning and commission of the murders which were committed in furtherance of a common design to forcibly take an unborn child from the mother who was nine months pregnant.

PEOPLE v. WILLIAMS
193 Ill.2d 306, 250 Ill.Dec. 692, 739 N.E.2d. 455, (2000)

[Case citations omitted.]

Justice McMORROW delivered the opinion of the court:

BACKGROUND

On November 16, 1995, Debra Evans was fatally shot and stabbed in the Addison apartment where she lived with James Edwards and her children, 10-year-old Samantha, 7-year-old Joshua, and Jordan who was almost 2 years old. Debra was nine months pregnant, and the baby she was carrying, Elijah Evans, was cut from her womb. Samantha was killed in the apartment with her mother. Joshua and Elijah were taken from the apartment, and Jordan was left alone in the apartment with his dead mother and sister. The day after Debra and Samantha were murdered, police found Joshua's dead body in an alley in Maywood. When police arrested defendant, Jacqueline Annette Williams, on November 17, she was holding Elijah, who was still alive. In connection with the murders and kidnappings of the members of the Evans family, the defendant, Jacqueline Annette Williams, her cousin Lavern Ward [who had children in common with Debra], and her boyfriend, Fedell Caffey, were jointly indicted on several counts of first degree murder and aggravated kidnapping. They were tried separately.

Following a jury trial in the Circuit Court of DuPage County, defendant was convicted of the first degree murders of Debra, Samantha, and Joshua Evans. She was also convicted of the aggravated kidnappings of Joshua and Elijah Evans. Defendant appealed her murder convictions and death sentence.

In a written statement, defendant...stated that she and Caffey had been dating for two years. Throughout their relationship, defendant and Caffey had attempted to conceive a child. Caffey wanted a baby boy with light skin so that the baby would resemble him.***

According to defendant's statement, Ward was upset with Debra during the four months that preceded the murders. On November 16, 1995, Ward, Caffey, and defendant drove to Debra's apartment...because Ward wanted to talk to Debra about their son Jordan.***

Defendant further stated that she, Caffey, and Ward arrived at Evans' apartment at about 9 p.m. Debra let them into the building and apartment. Debra sat on a small couch, and she and defendant had a conversation about their children. Subsequently, while defendant was in the bathroom, she heard a loud ringing noise. She exited the bathroom and saw Debra lying on her back. Debra's eyes were blinking rapidly, and bubbles were coming from her mouth. Caffey was holding a small silver automatic gun. Ward was standing beside Debra and appeared to be stabbing her in the neck.

Caffey then made a cut "crossways" on Debra's abdomen with poultry shears. As he cut, defendant could see the head of a baby. She and Caffey wanted the baby because it was a boy. Caffey pulled the baby from Debra and cut the umbilical cord while defendant stood next to him. Caffey did not want the baby at that point because he thought he had killed the baby, but defendant still wanted the baby. She blew into the baby's nose and mouth, and he began breathing.

Defendant further stated that, as she dressed the baby in a sleeper, Caffey and Ward went into the children's bedroom. Joshua ran from the bedroom crying that Caffey and Ward were hurting his sister. Defendant covered Debra with a blanket, but when Joshua saw his mother, he vomited and ran to the bathroom.

Defendant began to leave the apartment with the baby. Joshua grabbed her legs and said that he did not want to stay there because Caffey and Ward were bad. Defendant and Joshua exited the apartment through the back entrance. Caffey and Ward joined them in the car and they all drove to a location on Roosevelt Road, where Ward exited the car. Defendant and Caffey then drove to [defendant's friend] Scott's, where they left Joshua. Defendant lied and told Scott that Joshua's mother had been shot at a "drug spot."

On Friday morning, defendant returned to Scott's apartment and learned that Joshua had told Scott about the murders. Defendant knew at that point that they "were in deep trouble." She took Joshua....

According to defendant's written statement...[t]hey were all afraid that Joshua would identify them. Caffey told defendant to tie a scarf around Joshua's mouth, which she did. Ward left....Defendant asked Joshua to sit on the bed and tried to poison him by having him swallow "antiseptic." Caffey asked defendant to get a knife. Defendant did so and gave Caffey the knife. Joshua was screaming and frightened.***

Defendant further stated that they put Joshua in the car on the floor behind the driver's seat. Defendant sat in the driver's seat, and Caffey sat in the back seat. Caffey wrapped a cord around Joshua's neck several times and ordered defendant...to pull on the ends of the cord. Joshua was screaming, crying, and moaning. Defendant...dropped the cord, and Caffey began stabbing Joshua. Defendant drove to Maywood, where she pulled into an alley. She removed the sheet that was wrapped around Joshua and left him in the alley. Defendant dumped the sheet at a piano company....They killed Joshua because he knew who committed the murders.

ANALYSIS

According to defendant, her convictions for the murders of Debra and Samantha Evans must be reversed because there was no evidence that defendant inflicted any injuries to Debra or Samantha. Defendant further contends that the State failed to prove that she was accountable for Debra's and Samantha's murders because there was no evidence that she knew that Ward, Caffey, [or anyone else] went to the Evans apartment with the intent to commit a crime or that she joined this group with knowledge that criminal acts were going to occur. Defendant does not contend that there was insufficient evidence to support her conviction for Joshua's murder or her convictions for the aggravated kidnappings of Joshua and Elijah.***

Section 5-2(c) of the Criminal Code of 1961 provides that a person is legally accountable for the criminal conduct of another if "[e]ither before or during the commission of an offense, and with the intent to promote or facilitate such commission, he solicits, aids, abets, agrees or attempts to aid, such other person in the planning or commission of the offense." To prove that the defendant possessed the intent to promote or facilitate the crime, the State may present evidence which establishes beyond a reasonable doubt that (1) the defendant shared the criminal intent of the principal or (2) there was a common criminal design. A defendant's intent may be inferred from the nature of her actions and the circumstances accompanying the criminal conduct. Under the common-design rule, if "two or more persons engage in a common criminal design or agreement, any acts in the furtherance of that common design committed by one party are considered to be the acts of all parties to the design or agreement and all are equally responsible for the consequences of the further acts." Words of agreement are not needed to establish a common design; rather, like intent, a common design may be inferred from the circumstances surrounding the commission of the crime. Mere presence at a crime, even when combined with knowledge that a crime is being committed and flight from the scene, is insufficient to establish guilt by accountability. However, "[e]vidence that a defendant voluntarily attached himself to a group bent on illegal acts with knowledge of its design supports an inference that he shared the common purpose and will sustain his conviction for an offense committed by another.

CONCLUSION

...[W]e hold that a rational trier of fact could have found beyond a reasonable doubt that defendant was accountable for Debra's and Samantha's murders. Evidence presented at trial indicated that defendant aided and abetted Ward and Caffey in the planning and commission of Debra's and Samantha's murders and that these murders were committed in furtherance of a common design to take Elijah from Debra by force.

With respect to defendant's role in the planning and commission of the murders, there was testimony that, during the months that preceded the murders, defendant attempted to obtain a gun....One week before the murders, defendant visited Evans' apartment and asked Edwards when he left for work and how he traveled to work. Hours before the murders, defendant was seen having two conversations with Ward and Caffey. Defendant admitted in her written statement that she stood next to Caffey as he cut open Debra's abdomen, and there was medical testimony that more than one person would have been required to make the incision to her uterus and remove the baby. Further, a bloody Ace bandage was discovered in a bedroom in the Evans apartment. Edwards had not seen this bandage before, and defendant had been seen wearing an Ace bandage on her arm a few days before the murders.

Evidence of defendant's participation in a common design to take Elijah from Debra by force included testimony that Ward was Elijah's father; that Ward and Debra had argued about the baby's paternity; and that defendant knew that Ward and Caffey went to Evans' apartment to talk to Debra about the unborn baby and to "teach [her] a lesson." There was also evidence that defendant and Caffey wanted Elijah and planned to pretend he was their son. In her written statement, defendant admitted that she and Caffey wanted a light-skinned baby boy but had been unable to have one. Defendant knew that Debra had planned to enter the hospital to give birth on Monday, November 20. During the months that preceded the murders, defendant had made false claims that she was pregnant and indicated that her due date was in October, a few weeks before Debra was due to give birth. A few days before the murders, defendant told her probation officer that she had given birth to a baby named Elijah, the name that Debra had chosen for the child she was carrying. After the murders, defendant told her mother, sister, and police that Elijah was her son. Evidence of defendant's presence in Evans' apartment during the murders, her flight from the apartment with Ward and Caffey, her failure to report the murders to police, and her continued close affiliation with Caffey after the murders also supported a finding of common design. Based on this evidence, we believe a rational jury could have found defendant accountable for Debra's and Samantha's murders, and we reject defendant's challenge to the sufficiency of the evidence.

***

61

C. Critical Thinking

▶Under the common design rule, the defendant need only intend to aid the principal in one offense and does not have to intend to commit other crimes which may be committed by the principal in the commission of the intended offense. What do you believe was the defendant's intent when she went to the apartment that day?

E. Questions

Please choose the correct answer for the following questions.

1. The accountability theory:

a. is a separate crime
b. is the same as guilt by association
c. recognizes the same classifications of parties to a crime as the common law
d. is a method by which an individual may be held liable for an offense committed by another

2. Which of the following is a true statement regarding accountability?

a. the statute applies only to felony offenses
b. a "willing victim" of a criminal act will always be found equally liable
c. the accomplice must intend to aid in the commission of the offense
d. a defendant may not be found guilty under an accountability theory when the identity of the principal is unknown

3. A defendant may be held legally accountable for the criminal actions of another based upon:

a. the fact that defendant is present at the crime scene
b. defendant's knowledge that a crime was being committed
c. defendant's intentional participation in the commission of the crime
d. none of the above

4. Accountability may be established by showing the defendant:

a. aided in the commission of the offense
b. participated before or during the offense
c. intended to facilitate the commission of the offense
d. all of the above

5. When a defendant intends to aid in a crime, and then other criminal acts are committed in furtherance of that crime, the defendant:

a. will be liable only for the original crime
b. will be liable for any criminal act committed in furtherance of the intended crime
c. the State need only prove the defendant's intent to aid in one of the crimes
d. both b and c

CHAPTER SIX

Inchoate Offenses

An inchoate offense is one that is incomplete. Even though the defendant fails to complete all of the steps required for the intended crime, the defendant's actions will make him liable for some lesser crime under the law. Inchoate offenses consist of: solicitation, conspiracy, and attempt. Each of these offenses is preliminary to another, more serious offense.

On the issue of inchoate offenses, the tough questions for courts and counsel are: 1) when do the actions of the defendant cross the line between mere preparation and the actual beginning of the inchoate offense; and 2) when do the actions of the defendant cross the line between the inchoate offense and the intended crime? Illinois statutes defining inchoate offenses do not even try to cover every possible fact pattern, but rather, serve only as a guide to identifying possible circumstances under which these crimes may occur. Under Illinois law, no person shall be convicted of both the inchoate offense and the principal offense.

I. Solicitation

A. Comments

Common law had provided that any person counseling, advising or encouraging an infant under the age of ten years, a lunatic or idiot, to commit any offense should be prosecuted as a principal for such offense when committed, and punished the same as if he had committed the offense. The legislature agreed with this reasoning and made solicitation a statutory offense when common law offenses were abolished in Illinois.

The solicitation statute requires the offender have the specific intent to commit the principal offense, and then command, encourage or request another to commit the crime. The defendant who solicits another to commit a crime is looked upon with great disfavor under the law. The statute provides that the penalty for solicitation of a crime, other than first-degree murder, may be the same as for the intended offense, as long as it does not exceed the corresponding maximum sentence for an attempt.

Separate statutes exist for solicitation of murder and solicitation of murder for hire. Both statutes require the person possess the intent to commit a first-degree murder. While both statutes are a Class X felony, the maximum term of imprisonment for solicitation of murder for hire exceeds that of solicitation of murder. Individuals serving prison sentences for either of these offenses also have limitations placed on good conduct credit.

B. Statutes

720 ILCS 5/8-1 Solicitation

(a) Elements of the offense. A person commits solicitation when, with intent that an offense be committed, other than first degree murder, he commands, encourages or requests another to commit that offense.

(b) Penalty. A person convicted of solicitation may be fined or imprisoned or both not to exceed the maximum provided for the offense solicited: Provided, however, the penalty shall not exceed the corresponding maximum limit provided by subparagraph (c) of Section 8-4 of this Act [Attempt], as heretofore and hereafter amended.

720 ILCS 5/8-1.1 Solicitation of Murder

(a) A person commits solicitation of murder when, with the intent that the offense of first degree murder be committed, he commands, encourages or requests another to commit that offense.

(b) Penalty. Solicitation of murder is a Class X felony and a person convicted of solicitation of murder shall be sentenced to a term of imprisonment for a period of not less than 15 years and not more than 30 years, except that in cases where the person solicited was a person under the age of 17 years, the person convicted of solicitation of murder shall be sentenced to a term of imprisonment for a period of not less than 20 years and not more than 60 years.

720 ILCS 5/8-1.2 Solicitation of Murder for Hire

(a) A person commits solicitation of murder for hire when, with the intent that the offense of first degree murder be committed, he procures another to commit that offense pursuant to any contract, agreement, understanding, command or request for money or anything of value.

(b) Penalty. Solicitation of murder for hire is a Class X felony and a person convicted of solicitation of murder for hire shall be sentenced to a term of imprisonment of not less than 20 years and not more than 40 years.

720 ILCS 5/8-5 Multiple convictions

No person shall be convicted of both the inchoate and the principal offense.

720 ILCS 5/8-6 Offense

For the purposes of this Article, "offense" shall include conduct which if performed in another State would be criminal by the laws of that State and which conduct if performed in this State would be an offense under the laws of this State.

C. Case

In the following case, the defendant contends her sentence of 18 years' imprisonment for solicitation to commit murder violates the Illinois Constitution because it is harsher than a sentence would be for a conviction of either conspiracy to commit murder or attempted murder. In reaching a decision on defendant's appeal, the court compares the inchoate offenses of solicitation of murder, conspiracy to commit murder, and attempted murder.

PEOPLE v. KAUTEN
324 Ill.App.3d 588, 258 Ill.Dec. 197, 755 N.E.2d 1016 (2 Dist. 2001)

[Case citations omitted.]

Justice RAPP delivered the opinion of the court:

BACKGROUND

Defendant, Bonnie J. Kauten, pleaded guilty to solicitation of murder. In return, the State dismissed a charge of solicitation of murder for hire but made no sentencing concessions. The trial court sentenced defendant to 18 years' imprisonment and denied her motion to reconsider the sentence.

Defendant appeals, arguing that her sentence must be vacated because the sentencing scheme for solicitation of murder violates the proportionate penalties clause of the Illinois Constitution (Ill. Const.1970, art. I, § 11). Defendant maintains that the legislature has impermissibly penalized solicitation of murder more severely than what she claims are the more serious offenses of conspiracy to commit murder and attempted murder. We affirm.

ANALYSIS

The proportionate penalties clause commands that "All penalties shall be determined *** according to the seriousness of the offense ***." This clause bars different sentencing ranges for offenses with identical elements. It also forbids disproportionate punishments for similar but not identical offenses. Thus, the legislature may not prescribe a greater penalty for a less serious offense than it has for a more serious offense. In determining the seriousness of a given offense, the legislature may consider not only the degree of harm the offense inflicts but also the frequency of the crime and the need for a more stringent penalty to halt an upsurge in its frequency. The legislature is best situated to decide what conduct to criminalize and how severely to punish an offense. Therefore, courts normally defer to the legislature's conclusion that one offense is more serious than another.

A person commits solicitation of murder when, with the intent that the offense of first-degree murder be committed, he commands, encourages, or requests another to commit that offense. As pertinent here, solicitation of murder is a Class X felony punishable by 15 to 30 years' imprisonment.

A person commits conspiracy when, with the intent that an offense be committed, he or she agrees with another to the commission of that offense and either he or she or a coconspirator commits an act in furtherance of the agreement. The sentence for conspiracy to commit first-degree murder may not exceed that for a Class 2 felony, *i.e.*, 3 to 7 years' imprisonment. A person commits attempted murder when, with the intent to commit murder, he or she does any act constituting a substantial step toward the commission of that offense. Attempted first-degree murder is a Class X felony and, absent certain aggravating factors, is subject to the Class X sentencing range, 6 to 30 years' imprisonment.

As defendant notes, the penalty for solicitation of murder (15 to 30 years' imprisonment) is more severe than that for either conspiracy to commit first-degree murder (3 to 7 years' imprisonment) or attempted murder (6 to 30 years' imprisonment). Defendant asserts that these disparities are constitutionally impermissible. Defendant observes that the crime of solicitation of murder is complete when a person who has the requisite intent does no more than encourage or urge another to act. However, conspiracy to commit murder or attempted murder necessarily involves not only the same intent but also either an act by the defendant or a coconspirator in furtherance of the plan or a "substantial step" by the defendant toward committing the murder. Thus, defendant concludes, solicitation of murder is necessarily less serious than either conspiracy to commit murder or attempted murder and may not be punished more severely.

***

We first hold that the State may penalize solicitation of murder more severely than it penalizes conspiracy to commit murder.***[S]olicitation poses special dangers not inherent in conspiracy, one of which is that the instigator will be a sophisticated operator, such as a gang leader, who will hide behind his hireling(s). Laws against solicitation target those at the top of the proverbial totem pole. Thus, these laws play a distinctive and important role in suppressing organized crime.

...[S]olicitation cannot be considered the mere equal of conspiracy, as often a solicitation is the proximate *cause* of a conspiracy. A conspiracy takes place among those who already intend to bring about a crime, but a solicitation is an effort to recruit one who has not yet formed criminal intentions and to implant such intentions in his or her mind. A person who is afraid or unable to commit murder on his or her own may solicit the help of another (or many others) who would otherwise lack the incentive to commit murder. What neither would attempt individually may come about by their cooperation. Thus, many a solicitation creates a conspiracy where none existed before.

...We next hold that the State may punish solicitation of murder more severely than attempted murder.

First, almost by definition, a solicitation of murder will involve greater premeditation, planning, or criminal sophistication than will many attempted murders. ***Of course, not every solicitation of murder will be more sophisticated than every attempted murder. However, that is not necessary for the different punishments to represent a reasonable legislative judgment that satisfies the proportionate penalties clause.

Second, the solicitation of a murder may lead to an attempt at murder where no attempt would have been made otherwise. Indeed, one common purpose of asking someone else to commit a murder is to make the planned murder possible or practical. Solicitation of murder and attempted murder are not simply equivalent because the former often causes the latter. Thus, while both solicitation of murder and attempted murder endanger the potential victim, solicitation of murder also creates more potential victims.

As the foregoing analysis may suggest, a final consideration supports punishing solicitation of murder more severely than either conspiracy to commit murder or attempted murder. All of the laws under discussion here protect potential murder victims. However, unlike the laws against conspiracy or attempted murder, criminalizing the solicitation of murder protects vulnerable people from the corrupting or oppressive act of solicitation itself.

Courts elsewhere have held that a state may punish a solicitation that occurs within the state even though the contemplated crime is to be committed outside the state. In so holding, these courts have reasoned that a state is rightly concerned "not only with the prevention of the harm that would result should the inducements prove successful, but with *protecting inhabitants of [the] state from being exposed to inducements* to commit or join in the commission of the crimes specified." (Emphasis added.) We agree with this reasoning.

CONCLUSION

We conclude that criminalizing the solicitation of murder serves purposes beyond those served by laws against conspiracy to commit murder or attempted murder and in part serves to deter the formation of conspiracies or attempts. Often, a solicitation is the start of an enterprise that grows into a conspiracy or an attempt. The legislature could reasonably find that solicitation of murder is a more widespread, elusive, and intractable social ill than conspiracy to commit murder or attempted murder. Therefore, the scheme under which defendant was sentenced does not violate the proportionate penalties clause, and her sentence must stand.

The judgment of the Circuit Court of DuPage County is affirmed.

D. Critical Thinking

▶In the above case, the defendant agreed to plead guilty to solicitation of murder in exchange for the State's dismissal of the solicitation of murder for hire charge. How was that advantageous to the defendant?

▶The offense of solicitation occurs even if the person requested to commit the offense does not agree to perform. What argument would you make that solicitation poses a greater threat to the public than does conspiracy, where two or more persons must agree to commit the offense?

▶When a person solicits murder and his agent actually accomplishes that goal, Illinois courts have held that section 8-5 precludes that person from being convicted of both solicitation of murder and first-degree murder. What argument would you make in support of such a holding?

II. Conspiracy

A. Comments

Under common law, a conspiracy was simply an agreement to do any unlawful act. Historically, both statutory and common law conspiracies were punishable in Illinois. Today, Illinois law defines conspiracy as an agreement between two or more persons to do certain acts which are listed in the statute, with the intent that an offense be committed. There must be not only an intent to agree, but also an intent to commit the offense which is the object of the agreement. For a conviction, the prosecution must also prove there was at least one act in furtherance of the agreement committed by the defendant or by a co-conspirator. The agreement can be by words, acts, or understanding. Because of the secretive nature of a conspiracy, courts allow broad inferences to be drawn concerning a defendant's intent and agreement. Courts allow circumstantial evidence to be used to show a common criminal purpose.

The heart of the conspiracy is the agreement; therefore, the conspiracy itself is a crime whether or not the intended crime is accomplished. Once the agreement has been entered into, each co-conspirator is criminally liable for the acts of his co-conspirators which are done in furtherance of the object of the agreement. In other words, to be liable, co-conspirators need not take part in each and every one of the actions performed towards accomplishing the crime. While it takes at least two to conspire, it is not a defense that the person with whom the defendant is alleged to have conspired has not been prosecuted or convicted. Subsection (b) of the conspiracy statute addresses other circumstances that may not be used as a defense to the charge.

Even at common law, conspiracy required an agreement between at least two individuals. "Wharton's Rule" provided that an agreement by two individuals to commit a particular crime could not be prosecuted as a conspiracy when the crime necessarily required the participation of two people. Examples include soliciting for a prostitute, bribery, or an illegal drug transaction. Wharton's Rule has been abolished in Illinois. Subsection 8-2(a) of the conspiracy statute refers to an agreement to commit *any* offense. The fact that more than one person is required to commit a particular offense is even more reason to punish the preliminary agreement to commit the crime.

Generally, a person convicted of conspiracy may face the maximum sentence for the offense which is the object of the conspiracy. While subsection 8-2(c) of the statute below lists certain exceptions, a sentence for conspiracy corresponds to the seriousness of the principal offense.

B. Statute

720 ILCS 5/8-2 Conspiracy

(a) Elements of the offense. A person commits conspiracy when, with intent that an offense be committed, he agrees with another to the commission of that offense. No person may be convicted of conspiracy to commit an offense unless an act in furtherance of such agreement is alleged and proved to have been committed by him or by a co-conspirator.

(b) Co-conspirators. It shall not be a defense to conspiracy that the person or persons with whom the accused is alleged to have conspired:
(1) Has not been prosecuted or convicted, or
(2) Has been convicted of a different offense, or
(3) Is not amenable to justice, or
(4) Has been acquitted, or
(5) Lacked the capacity to commit an offense.

(c) Sentence. A person convicted of conspiracy may be fined or imprisoned or both not to exceed the maximum provided for the offense which is the object of the conspiracy, [except as otherwise prohibited.]

C. Case

In the following case, the Illinois Court of Appeals reversed defendant's convictions for bribery, official misconduct, and conspiracy. On the conspiracy charge, the court held that the State had failed to prove the defendant had the specific intent to commit conspiracy. Although the defendant made statements to investigators, the court found her statements could not be considered a confession. The court determined that defendant's statements were so vague as to time and relation to the particular events that they were meaningless. As you read the case, keep in mind that for a conspiracy, the agreement can be by words, acts, or understanding.

PEOPLE v. ADAMS
238 Ill.App.3d 733, 179 Ill.Dec. 747, 606 N.E.2d 579 (1 Dist. 1992)

[Case citations omitted.]

Justice CERDA delivered the opinion of the court:

BACKGROUND

In March 1987, after receiving a tip from Andrea Harris, an informant, about fictitious drivers' licenses allegedly being issued, the Illinois State Police initiated an investigation of the Secretary of State's drivers' license testing facility located at 99th Street and Martin Luther King Drive in Chicago. Five special agents participated in the investigation by visiting the facility with Harris on various occasions in an attempt to obtain fictitious drivers' licenses. The defendant, Judith Adams, worked at the facility as a clerk.

[The investigation revealed that the cost of a fictitious driver's license was $500. The operation's admitted bagman, James Cokely, would turn over the $500 from the "applicant" and the information for the driver's license to Eugene Richardson, defendant's supervisor. Cokely would usually get $75 for his efforts.

On June 22, 1987, one of the special agents, working undercover and wearing a body wire, went to the drivers' license facility where he met the operation's admitted bagman, James Cokely. The agent paid $500 to Cokely for a fictitious driver's license. Cokely took the agent to the vision counter where he introduced him to Richardson. After handing Richardson a piece of paper with the information for the fictitious driver's license, the agent observed Richardson go to the lobby. The agent saw Richardson speak with the defendant but could not hear the conversation. Richardson then told the agent to go to defendant to complete the application. The agent saw defendant with the paper that he earlier had given to Richardson.

The defendant requested identification from the agent three times. When he told her he did not have any identification, defendant filled out the application with the information that the agent gave her. The defendant asked the agent for his social security number. After giving five numbers, the agent told defendant that he could not remember the last four numbers. Defendant told him to make up some numbers. Defendant finished filling out the application and told the agent to go to the cashier.

Richardson motioned to the agent, gave him a completed written test, and told him to sit down and go through the motions. The agent was then instructed to go outside to take the road test. Without taking the test, he was told by Cokely to go back inside to have his picture taken. The agent then got his fictitious driver's license.

Subsequently in the investigation, defendant admitted she was periodically paid, usually $50, by Richardson and another supervisor to fill out information on applications without seeing proper identification. Defendant also stated she had no knowledge of fictitious driver's licenses, had no knowledge of any other employees receiving any money for giving any unauthorized assistance, and had never given or seen any employee give an improper exam. Defendant stated she completed the application on June 22nd without proper identification because she was afraid of being written up for insubordination by Richardson or the other supervisor. Defendant also stated that she never saw any money exchanged and she was unaware of any money being exchanged.

After a bench trial, defendant was convicted of two counts each of bribery, official misconduct, and conspiracy resulting from the sale of the fraudulent driver's license on June 22, 1987. She was sentenced to 30 months' probation and required to forfeit her public employment.

On appeal, defendant asserted, *inter alia*, that the State failed to prove her guilty of conspiracy since there was no evidence that she ever agreed to the scheme.]

ANALYSIS

Taking defendant's statement and the other evidence in the light most favorable to the prosecution, the State did not prove defendant guilty of bribery, official misconduct, and conspiracy beyond a reasonable doubt. Conspiracy is proved by showing (1) an intent to commit an offense; (2) an agreement with another to commit the offense; and (3) the commission of an act in furtherance of the agreement by a co-conspirator.

The State does not have to prove that the conspirators actually met and entered into a specific agreement. Instead, the agreement can be by words, acts, or understanding. Furthermore, through circumstantial evidence, conspiracy can be proven by showing a common criminal purpose. Even so, the State must prove that the accused had the specific intent to commit conspiracy.

CONCLUSION

The State did not prove defendant guilty of conspiracy because they did not prove that she agreed to the license-for-sale scheme or was a knowing participant in the ongoing operation or had the specific intent to commit conspiracy. Therefore, we reverse her convictions for conspiracy.

***

D. Critical Thinking

► Considering an agreement does not have to be by words, but may be established by acts or an understanding, what do you think the trial court relied upon in finding the defendant guilty of conspiracy in the license-for-sale scheme?

► What acts point to a conspiracy between Richardson and Cokely?

III. Attempt

A. Comments

The Illinois attempt statute pertains to an attempt to commit any offense. A person commits an attempt when, with intent to commit a specific offense, he does any act which constitutes a substantial step toward the commission of that offense. Under common law, a conviction required that the attempt fail. That is no longer the law in Illinois. Section 8-4(a) of the attempt statute abolished the element of failure in attempt. Naturally, should the attempt be successful, the attempt becomes an included offense of the principal offense. Should a person attempt to commit murder and the victim dies as a result, the perpetrator will not be prosecuted for a "successful" attempted murder as well as the murder itself.

The statute requires the perpetrator do some act which constitutes a substantial step toward the commission of the offense. Since the statute does not further define an act which constitutes a "substantial step," it may be difficult to determine when the perpetrator has crossed the line between mere preparation to commit the offense, which does not violate the statute, and an actual attempt to commit the crime. In determining what constitutes a substantial step toward commission of the offense, Illinois courts have considered acts which place the defendant in dangerous proximity to success in committing the offense. It is well recognized that while mere preparation is not a substantial step, the required act does not have to be the last deed immediately preceding successful completion of the crime. Courts must make this decision on a case-by-case basis.

Generally, a person convicted of an attempt faces the maximum sentence provided for the offense attempted. There are exceptions, as with the other inchoate offenses of solicitation and conspiracy, which are outlined in the statute below. A prisoner serving a sentence for attempt to commit first-degree murder will be limited in the amount of good conduct credit he may receive.

B. Statute

720 ILCS 5/8-4 Attempt

(a) Elements of the Offense. A person commits an attempt when, with intent to commit a specific offense, he does any act which constitutes a substantial step toward the commission of that offense.

(b) Impossibility. It shall not be a defense to a charge of attempt that because of a misapprehension of the circumstances it would have been impossible for the accused to commit the offense attempted.

(c) Sentence. A person convicted of an attempt may be fined or imprisoned or both not to exceed the maximum provided for the offense attempted but, except for an attempt to commit the offense [of Armed Violence],

***

(2) the sentence for attempt to commit a Class X felony is the sentence for a Class 1 felony;

(3) the sentence for attempt to commit a Class 1 felony is the sentence for a Class 2 felony;

(4) the sentence for attempt to commit a Class 2 felony is the sentence for a Class 3 felony; and

(5) the sentence for attempt to commit any felony other than those specified in Subsections (1), (2), (3) and (4) hereof is the sentence for a Class A misdemeanor.

C. Case

In the case below, the defendant, Shavun M. Hawkins, was tried for assaults on two different women on the same date, as well as a burglary charge. In addressing defendant's claim that he was not proved guilty of attempt criminal sexual assault, the court takes a close look at what acts constitute a substantial step toward commission of a criminal sexual assault.

PEOPLE v. HAWKINS
311 Ill.App.3d 418, 243 Ill.Dec. 621, 723 N.E.2d 1222 (4 Dist. 2000)

[Case citations omitted.]

Justice MYERSCOUGH delivered the opinion of the court:

BACKGROUND

After a bench trial in July 1997, defendant, Shavun M. Hawkins, was convicted of criminal sexual assault, attempt (criminal sexual assault), and residential burglary. On appeal, defendant claims *inter alia*, that he was not proved guilty of attempt (criminal sexual assault) beyond a reasonable doubt.

B.H. testified she was a student at Eastern Illinois University (Eastern) in May, 1996 and was living in a house... in Charleston with two of her sorority sisters, Dorothy and Rachel. Rachel's bedroom was in the basement, while B.H. and Dorothy each had a bedroom on the second floor. A sheet hung across the doorway to B.H.'s room because the upstairs bedrooms had no doors. The front door to the house did not have a working lock.

According to B.H.'s testimony, on May 30, 1996, B.H. and her roommates went to Mother's Bar where she had three vodka and cranberry juice drinks. B.H. was also taking Claritin D, an allergy medication, which caused her to feel "shaky and groggy." She last took the medication at 6 or 7 p.m. B.H. and her roommates socialized with other university students at the bar until it closed at 1 a.m. When they got home, B.H. immediately fell asleep on the couch in the living room on the main floor of the house.

B.H.'s roommates testified to what happened while B.H. slept. An impromptu "after bars" party commenced shortly after they got home, with 15 to 20 people in attendance. The party broke up at about 3 a.m.

B.H. testified she woke up at approximately 3:30 a.m. and was alone in the living room, where the lights were still on. She was unaware that a party had occurred or that one had been planned. After using the bathroom and pouring a class of lemonade, she went upstairs. On the way to her bedroom, she peeked into Dorothy's room and saw that she was not there. B.H. took some aspirin, went to her room, and got into bed without changing out of her sundress. She fell asleep immediately.

B.H. woke again at 4 or 4:15 a.m. to find defendant on top of her, kissing her on the mouth and having intercourse with her. When she realized what was happening, she told him to "get the f--- off of me" and pushed him away. He asked her if she was "sure." She rolled to the floor and got up. Her dress had been pulled up and her underpants were around her feet. Defendant's pants were around his ankles. No lights were on in the room, but ambient light came in from the hallway and streetlights that shined through the window. B.H. ran across the hall to Dorothy's room, turned on the light and tried to wake Dorothy. While B.H. was screaming to wake Dorothy, defendant stood at the doorway for approximately 15 seconds, then went downstairs. B.H. was able to see defendant more clearly at this point, as the lights were on.

On B.H.'s request, she was taken to her best friend's apartment. There, B.H. revealed what had happened and one of her friends called the police. An officer arrived and took a description of defendant from B.H. B.H. was then taken to a hospital.

S.G. was also a student at Eastern Illinois University. In May 1996, she was living in a townhouse in Charleston. S.G. and Kristin both had bedrooms in the basement, and Kristin had to walk through S.G.'s bedroom to get to her own. Three other people, including Jennifer and Bonnie, also lived in the house, occupying the upstairs bedrooms. The front door to the house was commonly left unlocked because friends of the residents frequently come and went.

S.G. testified she did homework until about 11:30 p.m. on May 30, 1996, then went to Mother's Bar. After she returned home, she did more schoolwork before retiring between 2 and 2:30 a.m. Kristin was not home at the time. S.G. slept in a single bed, positioned against a wall.

At approximately 5 a.m., S.G. heard someone (later identified as defendant) coming downstairs. She assumed it was Kristin. S.G. then heard what sounded like someone bumping into things and feeling around in the dark. She thought perhaps Kristin was drunk. Then defendant bumped the edge of S.G.'s bed, leaned against it, and felt along the top of the bed with his hands. At one point, he grabbed S.G.'s foot underneath the covers. Defendant then went to the light switch and turned it on and off again rapidly. The light flashed so quickly S.G. was not able to see anything. S.G. then felt defendant sit on the side of the bed and heard his shoelaces being untied and his shoes hitting the floor. He started to get under the covers when S.G. asked what was "going on." Defendant leaned over, put his arm on her shoulder and said "what's the matter baby, I came to kick it with you." S.G. sprung out of bed and turned on the light. She saw defendant, still sitting on the bed, wearing black pants and a white shirt, but with his shoes off. She asked him who he was and what he was doing there. He said his name was Shavun and someone had sent him to the house. S.G. did not understand what defendant said, so she asked him again. This time he said Kristin had sent him. S.G. went upstairs, screaming.

S.G. woke Jennifer first, then they both went into Bonnie's room, closed the door, and called the police. From inside the room they heard defendant leave the house. When the officer arrived, S.G. provided a description of the defendant. She had no recollection of having seen defendant before.

Two days after these incidents B.H. and S.G. picked defendant out of a photo lineup at the police station. Defendant was subsequently arrested and charged.

ANALYSIS

Defendant contends he was not proved guilty of attempt (criminal sexual assault) of S.G. beyond a reasonable doubt because, as a matter of law, his acts did not constitute a substantial step toward commission of a criminal sexual assault.

A person commits an attempt when, with intent to commit a specific offense, he does any act which constitutes a substantial step toward the commission of that offense. Determining when mere preparation to commit an offense ends, and perpetration of an offense begins, is one of the most "troublesome" areas in the law of inchoate offenses. Thus, what constitutes a substantial step is determined by the facts and circumstances of each particular case. Although the accused need not have completed the "last proximate act" to actual commission of a crime, mere preparation is not enough. A substantial step should put the accused in a "dangerous proximity to success."

The crime of attempt is complete upon the completion of a substantial step (with the requisite intent), and subsequent abandonment of the criminal purpose is no defense. Likewise, it is no defense to an attempt charge that because of a misapprehension of circumstances it would have been impossible for the accused to commit the offense attempted. Illinois courts have relied on the Model Penal Code for guidance in determining whether an accused has taken a substantial step toward commission of a crime. Under the Model Penal Code, an attempt has occurred when a person, acting with the required intent, "purposely does or omits to do anything which, under the circumstances as he believes them to be, is an act or omission constituting a substantial step in a course of conduct planned to culminate in his commission of the crime." The Model Penal Code lists types of conduct that *shall* not, as a matter of law, be held insufficient to support an attempt conviction, so long as the act is strongly corroborative of the actor's criminal purpose. The list includes the following:

"(a) lying in wait, searching for[,] or following the contemplated victim of the crime;
(b) enticing or seeking to entice the contemplated victim of the crime to go to the place contemplated for its commission;
(c) reconnoitering the place contemplated for the commission of the crime;
(d) unlawful entry of a structure, vehicle[,] or enclosure in which it is contemplated that the crime will be committed."

This list manifests the Model Penal Code's emphasis on the nature of steps taken, rather than on what remains to be done to commit a crime. [It is noted in this section of the Model Penal Code] "[t]hat further major steps must be taken before the crime can be completed does not preclude a finding that the steps already undertaken are substantial."

***

CONCLUSION

After careful consideration of the facts and circumstances of this case, the applicable statutes, precedent, and the Model Penal Code, we conclude that the evidence was sufficient to permit the trier of fact, here the judge, to conclude that defendant took a substantial step toward committing criminal sexual assault against S.G. The conduct at issue includes the following. Defendant had just been escorted out of B.H.'s house, where he had intercourse with B.H. while she slept. He unlawfully entered S.G.'s residence and proceeded to her bedroom. After fumbling around in the dark, defendant grabbed S.G.'s foot. He turned the light switch on and off. Defendant then sat on the edge of S.G.'s bed and removed his shoes. He started to get under the covers until he was interrupted by S.G.'s urgent request for an explanation. Defendant then put his arm on S.G.'s shoulder and told her he was there to "kick it" with her. Defendant did not leave until S.G. went upstairs screaming.

With these facts in evidence, the judge could reasonably conclude that defendant had crossed the line where preparation ends and actual execution of a criminal act begins. That defendant was merely preparing to commit a criminal sexual assault would be a reasonable conclusion had he been interrupted while looking for S.G.'s house; or upon entering the residence, in the absence of additional evidence corroborating his intent to commit a sexual assault. However, defendant's acts, specifically, sitting on S.G.'s bed, taking off his shoes, crawling between the sheets, and announcing his sexual object to "kick it" with her, were not only corroborative of his intent, but brought him within a "dangerous proximity of success" as well. Depending on what S.G. was wearing at the time (a fact not in the record), defendant may have been dangerously close to achieving sexual penetration....

An attempt crime is one "that falls short of completion through means other than the defendant's voluntary relenting." Defendant's "attempt" ended when S.G. stopped it by removing herself from the situation, not by defendant's volition. The trier of fact could reasonably conclude that, when defendant got into bed with S.G., he was past the point where he was likely to experience a change of heart.

***

D. Critical Thinking

▶ In the incident with the second woman, do you believe the appellate court gave sufficient consideration to the actions defendant points out he did *not* take in determining whether there had been a substantial step towards completion of the crime?

E. Questions

Please choose the correct answer for the following questions.

1. Which of the following offenses requires the defendant to command, encourage, or request another to commit a crime?

a. solicitation
b. conspiracy
c. attempt
d. all three offenses

2. Which of the following offenses requires an agreement as well as an act in furtherance of that agreement?

a. solicitation
b. solicitation of murder
c. conspiracy
d. attempt

3. Which of the following offenses requires a substantial step toward commission of the intended offense?

a. solicitation
b. solicitation of murder for hire
c. conspiracy
d. attempt

4. In Illinois, inchoate offenses:

a. are considered common law offenses
b. are failures to complete an intended crime
c. carry a maximum penalty of up to one year in jail
d. may be a misdemeanor or felony, but always carry a much lower penalty than for the intended offense

5. In order for a defendant to be convicted of conspiracy in Illinois:

a. Wharton's Rule must not be violated
b. all parties to the agreement must be prosecuted and convicted
c. the agreement must be in writing and signed by all parties
d. the defendant may not be convicted of the principal offense

CHAPTER SEVEN

Defenses to Criminal Liability: Justifiable Use of Force

I. Defense of Person

A. Comment

There is a large body of Illinois case law addressing the issue of self-defense, and when deadly force may be used. Generally, the law requires that: (1) the defendant must not be the aggressor; (2) there must be a real and immediate danger; (3) the force threatened must be unlawful; (4) the defendant believes the force used is necessary; and (5) that such belief is reasonable to protect either the defendant or another person. The use of deadly force is authorized only if defendant reasonably believes such force is necessary to prevent deadly force being used against himself or another.

A defense of justifiable use of force, such as self-defense is an affirmative defense. Should the defendant raise the defense of justifiable use of force at trial, and present some supporting evidence, the State then has the burden of proving the defendant guilty beyond a reasonable doubt as to that issue as well as the other elements of the offense.

B. Statutes

720 ILCS 5/7-1 Use of Force in defense of person

A person is justified in the use of force against another when and to the extent that he reasonably believes that such conduct is necessary to defend himself or another against such other's imminent use of unlawful force. However, he is justified in the use of force which is intended or likely to cause death or great bodily harm only if he reasonably believes that such force is necessary to prevent imminent death or great bodily harm to himself or another, or the commission of a forcible felony.

720 ILCS 5/7-14 Affirmative defense

A defense of justifiable use of force, or of exoneration, based on the provisions of this Article is an affirmative defense.

C. Case

The jury in the following case rejected defendant's claim of self-defense in the killing of another. It was up to the jury to determine whether defendant reasonably believed the danger he faced required the use of such force. As you read through the facts of the case, ask yourself how a reasonable person should have reacted.

PEOPLE v. MURILLO
225 Ill.App.3d 286, 167 Ill.Dec. 584, 587 N.E.2d 1199 (1 Dist. 1992)

[Case citations omitted.]

Justice GORDON delivered the opinion of the court:

BACKGROUND

Defendant Anibal Murillo was indicted for murder and found guilty by a jury of voluntary manslaughter and sentenced to 15 years' imprisonment. He appeals, contending *inter alia* that the State failed to prove that defendant's use of deadly force to defend himself from bodily harm and an attempted robbery was unreasonable.

On June 22, 1987, the defendant shot and killed Roberto "Beto" Romero in a gangway on West 21st Street in Chicago. The defendant claimed self-defense. Evidence introduced at trial included the testimony of Gregory Carrizales who stated that at about 11 p.m. on the night of the incident, he was on the front steps of 2855 West 21st Street in Chicago, talking with his friend Rudy Romero (the nephew of Roberto Romero), when he heard a chain link fence rattling. He described the noise as though someone was trying to jump over the fence or someone was getting pushed into it.

Carrizales saw defendant, whom he knew only by the nickname "Dillinger," 50 to 60 feet away shooting a gun into a gangway between two houses. When Carrizales first saw him, the defendant was taking steps back out of the gangway. Defendant fired three shots, the second two in faster succession than the first. Carrizales said the defendant was holding the gun with both arms extended forward. After firing the shots, defendant turned towards Carrizales and Rudy, and Carrizales ran into the house. When Carrizales went back outside, he saw Rudy and another individual standing in the gangway where they had seen the shots fired. Rudy told him that his [Rudy's] uncle had been shot.

Officer Frank Luera of the Chicago Police Department testified that he arrested defendant at defendant's home a block away from the incident less than an hour after the shooting. Defendant told the police he had no knowledge of the shooting, that he did not participate in it, and that he was playing basketball with a friend at the playground at the time of the shooting. Shortly after arriving home, the police arrived and arrested him. Defendant also told police that some days before the shooting, "Beto" Romero had taken a gold chain or medallion from him.

The defendant testified at his trial. He stated that approximately a week before the incident, the victim approached him and asked him for money. Defendant told him that he had none. Defendant noticed a pistol "right on him in his waistline." The victim pushed the defendant against a brick fence and took his gold St. Ignacius medal and his wallet and money. Immediately thereafter, defendant stopped a passing paddy wagon, and told the police what had happened. The victim told the police that he was just playing around, that defendant overreacted, and then returned the wallet and money. Neither the pistol nor the medallion was found.

Following that event, defendant bought a gun, even though he had been previously given a conditional discharge for a robbery conviction and knew that carrying a weapon was a violation of the terms of his discharge. Defendant said that he feared for his safety and of being robbed again.

Continuing his testimony, defendant stated that on June 22, 1987, he was walking down 21st Street on the way to visit a friend, when the victim grabbed him and threw him into the gangway against a fence. The victim asked him for money, and when defendant said he did not have any, the victim tried to reach into defendant's pockets. Defendant pulled away, and the victim pulled out a chrome pistol. Defendant already had his pistol out, and headed for the stairs to the gangway. When he reached the first step, he fired his weapon at the victim. Thinking he had missed the victim, he turned around and fired two more times. Defendant said he shot because he thought the victim was going to kill him. After firing the shots, the defendant ran towards the next gangway and through an alley. He threw his gun away as he was running, and went home.

Defendant admitted that he did not initially tell the police that he had shot in self-defense. He explained that he was afraid of going to jail for violating the terms of his conditional discharge by having a gun. Four witnesses were presented by the defendant at trial who testified to prior violent encounters with the victim. The autopsy indicated the victim was 6 feet tall and weighed 280 pounds.

The jury found defendant guilty of voluntary manslaughter, and the court sentenced him to 15 years' imprisonment. Defendant now appeals.

ANALYSIS

In order to legally justify a killing on the basis of self-defense, a defendant must have been acting under a reasonable belief that the use of force which was intended or likely to cause death or great bodily harm was necessary to prevent imminent death or great bodily harm to himself.

The following elements must each be present: (1) force has been threatened against the person; (2) the threatened person is not the aggressor; (3) the danger of harm is imminent; (4) the force threatened is unlawful; and (5) the defendant must reasonably believe that danger exists, and that countering it requires force, and the force required is the kind and amount of force used by the defendant.

When a defendant raises the issue of self-defense and introduces some evidence of each of these elements, the burden shifts to the State to prove beyond a reasonable doubt that the defendant did not act in self-defense. If the State negates any one of the elements beyond a reasonable doubt, it has met its burden and the defense must be rejected.

Defendant maintains that his unrebutted testimony establishes each of these elements. Romero grabbed the defendant, threw him against a fence and threatened him with a pistol. Romero was a large man, 6 feet tall weighing 280 pounds, with a reputation as a violent man. Romero was known to carry a gun, and had robbed the defendant just a week before the killing.

The trier of fact, however, need not accept as true the defendant's testimony regarding the incident and the necessity for self-defense. It is for the trier of fact to weigh the evidence and consider the probability or improbability of the defendant's testimony, the testimony of other witnesses and the circumstances of the killing.

Contrary to defendant's assertion, there is evidence in the record sufficient to rebut his testimony and provide a justifiable basis for the jury's finding that his belief at the time he fired the shots was unreasonable. The victim was shot three times. Two of the shots were to the victim's back, and took an upward path. From this, the jury could infer that those shots were fired when the victim was facing away from the defendant and was either already down or in the process of falling down. Moreover, the last two shots were fired after the defendant had escaped the victim's grasp and had moved to a distance of some five feet from the victim. Thus, even if the victim had originally threatened defendant as defendant claims, at this point, with his back to the defendant and while already on the ground or in the process of falling down, the victim no longer posed a threat to the defendant. "[T]he use of deadly force generally cannot be justified once the aggressor has been disabled or disarmed." "If one responds with such excessive force that one is no longer acting in self-defense but in retaliation, such excessive use of force renders one the protagonist; a non-aggressor has a duty not to become the aggressor."

In addition, although defendant testified that "Beto" pulled a gun, no gun was found. The failure to find a gun at the scene does not necessarily establish that defendant's fear of imminent harm was unreasonable, since it is not necessary for the victim to have actually possessed a weapon in order to justify a killing in self-defense. Here, however, defendant testified to the fact that the victim actually threatened him with a drawn pistol. Therefore, the fact that no gun was found is relevant towards materially impeaching defendant's version of the facts which he presented to justify a claim of self-defense.

Defendant also testified that when the victim pulled his gun, the defendant already had his gun out. "[O]ne cannot 'initially provoke the use of force against himself, with the intent to use such force as an excuse to inflict bodily harm upon the assailant."

The reasonableness of a defendant's belief that the danger he faced required force in response is a question of fact to be resolved by the trier of fact. On review, we will not disturb the determination of the trier of fact on a self-defense issue "unless the evidence is so unsatisfactory as to justify a reasonable doubt as to guilt."

CONCLUSION

For the reasons discussed above, we cannot say that the evidence is so unsatisfactory to raise a reasonable doubt as to whether defendant acted in self-defense, and therefore we shall not disturb the jury's determination of that issue.***

D. Critical Thinking

▶ Romero, the victim, had a reputation as a violent man who was known to carry a gun. No gun was found at the scene. Had the victim been in possession of a gun, what could have happened to it?

▶ Had a gun been found at the scene, do you think that would have been sufficient in the minds of the jury to justify defendant's self-defense claim?

▶ Assuming defendant's testimony regarding the incident is accurate, how do you think a "reasonable person" should have reacted?

II. Defense of Dwelling and Other Property

A. Comment

Illinois law has long separated the offenses of defense of dwelling and defense of other property. A person may forcefully prevent the unlawful entry of another into a residence whether or not the unlawful entry is being made with force. As with defense of person, the use of deadly force is limited to situations where it is reasonably believed that deadly force is a necessary response to a forcible felony, or a violent entry with a threat of personal violence to someone in the residence. The person employing such force need not be the person who lives in the residence, nor is there a requirement that the person retreat before using such force.

The use of force with regard to defense of real and personal property is more limited than that of a dwelling. While a person may use such force reasonably believed necessary to protect the property, deadly force may be used only to prevent a forcible felony.

B. Statutes

720 ILCS 5/7-2 Use of force in defense of dwelling

A person is justified in the use of force against another when and to the extent that he reasonably believes that such conduct is necessary to prevent or terminate such other's unlawful entry into or attack upon a dwelling. However, he is justified in the use of force which is intended or likely to cause death or great bodily harm only if:

(a) The entry is made or attempted in a violent, riotous, or tumultuous manner, and he reasonably believes that such force is necessary to prevent an assault upon, or offer of personal violence to, him or another then in the dwelling, or

(b) He reasonably believes that such force is necessary to prevent the commission of a felony in the dwelling.

720 ILCS 5/7-3 Use of force in defense of other property

A person is justified in the use of force against another when and to the extent that he reasonably believes that such conduct is necessary to prevent or terminate such other's trespass on or other tortuous or criminal interference with either real property (other than a dwelling) or personal property, lawfully in his possession or in the possession of another who is a member of his immediate family or household or of a person whose property he has a legal duty to protect. However, he is justified in the use of force which is intended or likely to cause death or great bodily harm only if he reasonably believes that such force is necessary to prevent the commission of a forcible felony.

C. Case

In the following case, the only issue before the Illinois Supreme Court was whether the State proved beyond a reasonable doubt that the defendant was not justified in using deadly force in the defense of a dwelling when he stabbed another to death. In the court's analysis, pay particular attention to the distinction drawn between self-defense and defense of a dwelling.

PEOPLE v. SAWYER
115 Ill.2d 184, 104 Ill.Dec. 774, 503 N.E.2d 331 (1986)

[Case citations omitted.]

Justice MORAN delivered the opinion of the court:

BACKGROUND

The defendant, Terrance Sawyer, was convicted by a McDonough County jury of voluntary manslaughter for the stabbing death of Garry Kennedy. The trial court, however, found that it had improperly refused to give the defendant's tendered instruction on the use of force in defense of a dwelling, and granted the defendant's motion for a new trial. At the retrial, a second jury convicted the defendant of voluntary manslaughter. The trial court sentenced the defendant to the minimum term of four years' imprisonment. The appellate court affirmed. We allowed the defendant's petition for leave to appeal.

The defendant and Kennedy had been acquainted for eight or nine years. They attended the same high school and had played basketball together. The defendant met Belinda Stevens while the two were students at Western Illinois University in Macomb. They started dating, and Stevens later gave birth to his child. After the child was born, the defendant, Stevens and their child lived together in Macomb. When the couple began having difficulties in their relationship, Stevens and the child moved to another apartment. Several months after she stopped living with the defendant, Stevens began dating Kennedy on occasion. While she was dating Kennedy, however, she continued to see the defendant from time to time. The defendant graduated from Western and moved back to his home in Chicago.

On September 18, 1983, the defendant drove from Chicago to Stevens' residence in Macomb. He was staying with Stevens on September 20, 1983, when, at approximately 10 p.m., Kennedy arrived. The defendant answered the door and let him inside, whereupon Kennedy, Stevens and the defendant briefly discussed their relationship. When Kennedy asked Stevens to choose between the defendant and himself, Stevens chose the defendant.

Kennedy asked Stevens why she chose the defendant. When Stevens explained that she did so because he could provide for her and her child, Kennedy slapped her. Kennedy then apologized and Stevens asked him to leave. As they approached the front door, Kennedy turned to Stevens, said, "You b----," and hit her again. Kennedy left the house.

The defendant entered the room, saw Stevens lying on the floor and said "What the f---" or "What the f--- [is] going on here." The defendant walked quickly to the kitchen and grabbed a knife. The defendant put the knife on a desk in the hallway near the front door and followed Kennedy outside.

86

The two men talked for about five minutes. Kennedy saw Stevens standing in the door, he asked her what she was looking at and started toward the house. The defendant said that when Stevens asked Kennedy not to enter the house, Kennedy replied, "You can't stop me," and entered the house. The defendant claimed that Kennedy pushed past Stevens and grabbed him. During the ensuing struggle, the defendant said he reached behind himself and found the knife he had placed on the desk earlier. He closed his eyes and struck out, stabbing Kennedy. Kennedy died from the stab wound to his chest a short time later.

ANALYSIS

The use of deadly force in defense of a dwelling is justified only when two factors are present. First, the victim's entry must be made in a "violent, riotous, or tumultuous manner." Second, the defendant's subjective belief that deadly force is necessary to prevent an assault upon, or an offer of personal violence to, himself or another in the dwelling must be reasonable. The defendant argues that both of these factors were present in his case.

Defendant first contends that Kennedy's reentry into the house was violent, riotous and tumultuous. To support this argument, he notes that Kennedy had slapped Stevens twice before he reentered the house, shouted profanity at her and ignored her request not to reenter the house. On the other hand, the record shows that although Kennedy had slapped Stevens twice, the defendant knew only that Kennedy had slapped her once. There was no struggle as Kennedy and the defendant came through the door. The evidence presented clearly established that Kennedy's reentry into Stevens' house was unlawful. We do not, however, believe that Kennedy entered in a "violent, riotous or tumultuous manner." The record shows that Kennedy simply opened the screen door and stepped inside the house.

Defendant also contends that he reasonably believed that deadly force was necessary to prevent an assault by Kennedy upon Stevens. In the context of self-defense, it is the defendant's perception of the danger, and not the actual danger, which is dispositive. Defense of dwelling differs from self-defense in that, unlike self-defense, defense of a dwelling "does not require danger to life or great bodily harm in order to invoke the right to kill." Nevertheless, as in cases of self-defense, the issue in defense of a dwelling is whether the facts and circumstances induced a reasonable belief that the threatened danger, whether real or apparent, existed....

The defendant argues that he reasonably believed that Kennedy was about to assault Stevens when he entered the house. In support of this argument, he claims that the evidence showed that Kennedy attempted to strike Stevens after he reentered the house. He claims...that Kennedy was the aggressor, was intoxicated, and had a history of violence which was known to the defendant. The record, however, fails to support the reasonableness of defendant's fear.

... While defendant contends that he feared Kennedy because he knew Kennedy to have carried a gun, this fear did not prevent the defendant from letting Kennedy inside the house when he answered the door. Nor did it prevent him from following Kennedy outside the house after he had slapped Stevens.... We believe the jury could have properly concluded, from the evidence, that the defendant could not have reasonably believed that Kennedy was about to assault or offer personal violence to himself or anybody else....

CONCLUSION

Our review of the record indicates that there was sufficient evidence for the jury to reject the defendant's claim that he reasonably believed that he was justified in using deadly force in defense of a dwelling. We believe, from the evidence presented, the jury could have properly concluded that the defendant's belief that Kennedy was about to commit an assault was unreasonable. Moreover, even if the jury found that the defendant reasonably believed that Kennedy was about to commit an assault, it could have properly found that the defendant's belief that the stabbing was necessary to prevent such an assault was unreasonable. Consequently, the evidence proved the defendant guilty of voluntary manslaughter beyond a reasonable doubt.

**

III. Use of Force in Arrest Situations

A. Comment

A law enforcement officer, in making a lawful arrest, may use whatever non-deadly force is needed to complete the arrest. Should the individual resist arrest, the officer is not required to retreat. The officer's right to use deadly force is limited to situations where the person to be arrested has caused or threatened great bodily harm, is using a deadly weapon in an attempt to escape, or the safety of others is threatened if the arrest is not made immediately. Naturally, an officer may act in self-defense as well as a citizen.

Common law permitted an officer to use deadly force to apprehend a fleeing felon. Consider however, that generally, common law felonies carried the death penalty. Former Illinois law permitted the use of deadly force in apprehending a fleeing felon as long as the officer first used all reasonable efforts to make the arrest without success. This law would have been similar to the statute at issue in the *Tennessee v. Garner* case referred to in the web exercise for this chapter.

Note that Illinois law does not allow a person to use force to resist arrest, even if the person believes the arrest is unlawful. Even if the arrest is unlawful, there are constitutional and statutory safeguards in place today, which did not exist under common law, which far outweigh the risks involved in forcibly resisting arrest.

B. Statutes

720 ILCS 5/7-5 Peace officer's use of force in making arrest

(a) A peace officer, or any person whom he has summoned or directed to assist him, need not retreat or desist from efforts to make a lawful arrest because of resistance or threatened resistance to the arrest. He is justified in the use of any force which he reasonably believes to be necessary to effect the arrest and of any force which he reasonably believes to be necessary to defend himself or another from bodily harm while making the arrest. However, he is justified in using force likely to cause death or great bodily harm only when he reasonably believes that such force is necessary to prevent death or great bodily harm to himself or such other person or when he reasonably believes both that:

(1) Such force is necessary to prevent the arrest from being defeated by resistance or escape; and

(2) The person to be arrested has committed or attempted a forcible felony which involves the infliction or threatened infliction of great bodily harm or is attempting to escape by use of a deadly weapon, or otherwise indicates that he will endanger human life or inflict great bodily harm unless arrested without delay.

(b) A peace officer making an arrest pursuant to an invalid warrant is justified in the use of any force which he would be justified in using if the warrant were valid, unless he knows that the warrant is invalid.

720 ILCS 5/7-7 Private person's use of force in resisting arrest

A person is not authorized to use force to resist an arrest which he knows is being made either by a peace officer or by a private person summoned and directed by a peace officer to make the arrest, even if he believes that the arrest is unlawful and the arrest in fact is unlawful.

720 ILCS 5/7-8 Force likely to cause death or great bodily harm

(a) Force which is likely to cause death or great bodily harm, within the meaning of Sections 7-5 and 7-6 includes:

(1) The firing of a firearm in the direction of the person to be arrested, even though no intent exists to kill or inflict great bodily harm; and

(2) The firing of a firearm at a vehicle in which the person to be arrested is riding.

(b) A peace officer's discharge of a firearm using ammunition designed to disable or control an individual without creating the likelihood of death or great bodily harm shall not be considered force likely to cause death or great bodily harm within the meaning of Sections 7-5 and 7-6.

C. Web Activity

No discussion of the constitutionality of the use of deadly force by police officers is complete without addressing the decision of the U.S. Supreme Court in the case of *Tennessee v. Garner*. Find the case at the URL below and answer the following questions:

URL:
http://caselaw.lp.findlaw.com/scripts/getcase.pl?navby=case&court=us&vol=471&page=1

▶ If facts identical to those in *Tennessee v. Garner* were before an Illinois trial court today, applying the law in 720 ILCS 5/7-5, what would be the likely ruling of the court?

▶ What lawful options would be available to an officer attempting to apprehend a suspect in such a situation?

IV. Necessity

A. Comment

The defense of necessity is long-standing, if not well-defined by statute. The factfinder will determine the reasonableness of the defense. Imagine a snowmobiler in an isolated area who becomes separated from his friends. He accidentally runs into a tree at dusk. Injured and with his machine disabled, he hobbles to a nearby cabin. Facing death or great bodily harm from exposure, he opts to break into the locked cabin to build a fire with the wood stored inside and await rescue. The owners of the cabin insist he be charged with burglary. Should a charge be filed, the hapless snowmobiler will certainly pursue a defense of necessity at trial.

B. Statute

720 ILCS 5/7-13 Necessity

Conduct which would otherwise be an offense is justifiable by reason of necessity if the accused was without blame in occasioning or developing the situation and reasonably believed such conduct was necessary to avoid a public or private injury greater than the injury which might reasonably result from his own conduct.

C. Case

In the case below, the defendant, an inmate at the Stateville Correctional Center in Joliet, appealed his conviction for escape contending he should have been allowed to present an affirmative defense of necessity. The Court of Appeals reversed the defendant's conviction, finding the trial court abused its discretion.

PEOPLE v. MUSGROVE
313 Ill.App.3d 217, 246 Ill.Dec. 214, 729 N.E.2d 865 (3 Dist. 2000),
appeal denied, 191 Ill.2d 551, 250 Ill.Dec. 464, 738 N.E.2d 933 (2000)

[Case citations omitted.]

Justice HOMER delivered the opinion of the court:

After a stipulated bench trial, the defendant was convicted of the offense of escape, and sentenced to six years in prison. On appeal, he contends that the trial court erred in: (1) granting the State's motion *in limine* which barred him from presenting the affirmative defense of necessity, and (2) denying his motion to represent himself. After our careful review, we reverse and remand the case for a new trial.

BACKGROUND

During all times relevant, the defendant was serving a 50-year sentence at Stateville Correctional Center for his 1989 convictions for murder, attempted armed robbery, unlawful use of a weapon, and conspiracy. While incarcerated, the defendant was charged by indictment with the offense of forgery for allegedly engaging in a scheme to defraud inmates at other correctional institutions. The defendant allegedly sent letters to these inmates on altered law firm stationery indicating that they had been awarded $2,500 in a class action settlement, which they could collect if they sent $25 to the defendant's post office box.

On April 22, 1997, the defendant was transported to the Will County courthouse by Officer Timms, an employee of the Illinois Department of Corrections (D)C), for an appearance on the forgery charge. As they prepared to leave, the defendant escaped from the back of the prison van before Officer Timms could close the door. After a brief foot chase, Officer Timms caught the defendant and placed him back into custody. The defendant was subsequently charged by indictment with the offense of escape.

Prior to trial on the escape charge, the defendant indicated that he intended to present the affirmative defenses of necessity and compulsion. He claimed that his life was in danger at Stateville because of the publicity surrounding the forgery case. The State filed a motion *in limine*, seeking to bar the defendant from presenting those defenses, which the trial court granted.

There were numerous delays in the proceedings. Thereafter, the defendant, who was represented by the public defender's office, requested that he be allowed to represent himself at trial. The trial judge denied his motion, finding that it was made too late and would further delay the trial. The case proceeded to a stipulated bench trial. After stipulating to the facts, the defendant was given the opportunity to make an offer of proof on the affirmative defense issues.

The defendant showed that after his indictment on the fraud charge, an article appeared in *The Joliet Herald News* identifying the defendant by name and describing his alleged scheme to defraud fellow inmates. The defendant testified that he first saw the article when it was posted on the bulletin board in the law library at Stateville in late 1996. Thereafter, he claims that he began receiving death threats and threats of physical harm from other inmates. He did not specifically know the names of the inmates, but knew some by their nicknames, gang affiliations, and job assignments. He stated that inmates had thrown urine and hot water on him and tried to strike him with broomsticks as he walked by the cells. The defendant's fellow inmate, Miles Barnes, testified that he was aware that the defendant had been threatened by inmates, but he had no information about specific threats.

The defendant stated that he first reported the threats to the warden and the assistant Director of Corrections in December, 1996. In January, 1997, the defendant filed a grievance that detailed his safety concerns and requested that the matter be handled as an emergency. The defendant's request for emergency status was denied. In the following months, the defendant wrote numerous letters regarding his safety concerns which he contends garnered no response. He stated that the purpose behind his escape attempt was to get the attention of the Department of Corrections officials. The defendant asserted that he had no intention of getting away, but he wanted to bring to their attention his serious safety concerns and his need to be protected and moved from Stateville.

At the conclusion of his offer of proof, the defendant was found guilty of escape and sentenced to six years in prison to be served consecutively to his current term. The defendant's post-trial motion was denied, and this appeal followed.

ANALYSIS

Necessity involves a choice that can only be made between two admitted evils, other options being unavailable. Even slight evidence of the forcing of this choice is sufficient to make the defense an issue for the trier of fact.

The following factors have been deemed valuable in assessing claims of necessity in escape cases:

"(1) The prisoner is faced with a specific threat of death, forcible sexual attack or substantial bodily injury in the immediate future;

(2) There is no time for a complaint to the authorities or there exists a history of futile complaints which make any result from such complaints illusory;

(3) There is no time or opportunity to resort to the courts;

(4) There is no evidence of force or violence used towards prison personnel or other 'innocent' persons in the escape; and

(5) The prisoner immediately reports to the proper authorities when he has attained a position of safety from the immediate threat."

All of these factors need not be present to establish necessity, and the absence of one or more does not necessarily prohibit the assertion of the defense. Rather, these factors are most useful in assessing the weight and credibility of the defendant's claim.

The instant defendant argues that the trial court erred in denying him the opportunity to present evidence to a jury on the defense of necessity. After our careful review, we agree.

Because there is very little information about the underlying forgery charge in the record, the defendant pleaded not guilty to the charge, and the charge remained pending at the time of the instant trial, we are unable to conclude that the defendant was to blame in occasioning or developing this situation. Further, the defendant has presented some evidence indicating that he reasonably believed that his actions were necessary to avoid great injury.

Specifically, the defendant testified that he received numerous threats of death and bodily harm from other prisoners in the months leading up to his escape attempt. He said that he feared for his life every waking minute and believed that an attack was imminent based upon the threats, gang activity, and level of hostility in Stateville. He testified that he made numerous complaints to DOC officials about the threats and assaults, but no action was ever taken to ensure his safety. The defendant admitted that he never told the judge about the threats during his numerous court appearances on the forgery charge, but based upon his knowledge of the procedures for complaints and grievances in the prison system, he believed that the judge could have done nothing about the situation anyway.

Further, the record shows that the defendant used minimal force in making his escape. Once recaptured within minutes of his escape, the defendant told Officer Timms that he had to make the escape because his life was threatened. The defendant stated that he had no intention of getting away, he just wanted to bring attention to his concerns for his own safety.

In response, the State argues, *inter alia*, that as an inmate of the segregation unit at Stateville, the defendant is confined to his cell 23 hours a day and has no cellmate, implying that there was no opportunity for the defendant to be threatened or harmed while incarcerated. However, the defendant testified that there were numerous opportunities for inmates to threaten and harm him as he walked past the cells and spent time in the library and prison yard. The State's assertions challenge the weight, credibility, and overall sufficiency of the evidence which are issues to be resolved when the evidence is presented at trial.

CONCLUSION

After our careful review of the record, we determine that there was sufficient evidence to permit the defendant to proceed to trial with his claim of necessity. Because the trial court erred in granting the State's motion *in limine*, we reverse the defendant's conviction and sentence and remand the cause for a new trial.

For the foregoing reasons, the judgment of the circuit court of Will County is reversed and the cause is remanded for a new trial.

D. Critical Thinking

▶ On the escape charge, assuming the defendant is given an opportunity to present the defense of necessity at trial, what do you believe the outcome will be? Why?

▶ If the defendant were convicted on the forgery charge prior to retrial on the escape, do you believe the factfinder would consider defendant "was without blame in occasioning or developing the situation" as required by the necessity statute?

E. Questions

Please choose the correct answer for the following questions.

1. Which of the following is a true statement?

a. the circumstances under which an individual may use deadly force to protect his person, his dwelling, or other property are identical
b. self-defense is an affirmative defense
c. the person who initiates the fight may rely on self-defense at trial
d. when confronted with force, the defendant may lawfully respond with excessive force

2. Which of the following is a true statement?

a. deadly force may not be used in defense of property
b. deadly force may be used to prevent any entry into a dwelling
c. deadly force may be used to prevent the commission of a felony inside a dwelling
d. deadly force may be used to prevent a trespass upon real property other than a dwelling

3. Which of the following is a true statement?

a. in making an arrest, an officer threatened with great bodily harm may lawfully utilize deadly force
b. an officer may use deadly force to seize a non-dangerous fleeing felon
c. a person who knows they are being arrested unlawfully may use force to resist the arrest
d. common law did not allow a peace officer to use deadly force to seize a suspected felon

4. The defense of necessity is justified where:

a. defendant did not intentionally create the situation
b. defendant reasonably believed his action necessary to avoid a greater evil
c. both a & b
d. neither a nor b

5. The defense of necessity:

a. is defined in great detail by statute
b. is new to Illinois law
c. both a & b
d. neither a nor b

CHAPTER EIGHT

Defenses to Criminal Liability: Excuses

I. Insanity and Mental Illness

A. Comment

Legal insanity differs from bizarre or antisocial behavior in its definition. Insanity, as a defense, requires the defendant show he lacked substantial capacity to appreciate the criminality of his conduct due to a mental disease or defect. The defendant must present some evidence at trial that tends to establish he was insane at the time the crime was committed. The prosecutor then has the burden of proving the defendant guilty beyond a reasonable doubt as to that issue as well as the other elements of the offense. It is up to the factfinder to determine whether the defendant will be held criminally responsible for his conduct.

When the defense of insanity is presented at trial, the court will determine whether it is appropriate for the jury to also consider a verdict of guilty, but mentally ill. While "insanity" is an actual defense, "mental illness" is not. At the time the crime was committed, the defendant may have been suffering from a mental illness which impaired his judgment, but was legally sane. In that case, the defendant will not be relieved of criminal responsibility for his behavior. The judge will, however, take defendant's mental illness into consideration when imposing the sentence.

B. Statutes

720 ILCS 5/6-2 Insanity

(a) A person is not criminally responsible for conduct if at the time of such conduct, as a result of mental disease or mental defect, he lacks substantial capacity to appreciate the criminality of his conduct.

(b) The terms "mental disease or mental defect" do not include an abnormality manifested only by repeated criminal or otherwise antisocial conduct.

(c) A person who, at the time of the commission of a criminal offense, was not insane but was suffering from a mental illness, is not relieved of criminal responsibility for his conduct and may be found guilty but mentally ill.

(d) For purposes of this Section, "mental illness" or "mentally ill" means a substantial disorder of thought, mood, or behavior which afflicted a person at the time of the commission of the offense and which impaired that person's judgment, but not to the extent that he is unable to appreciate the wrongfulness of his behavior.

(e) When the defense of insanity has been presented during the trial, the burden of proof is on the defendant to prove by clear and convincing evidence that the defendant is not guilty by reason of insanity. However, the burden of proof remains on the State to prove beyond a reasonable doubt each of the elements of each of the offenses charged, and, in a jury trial where the insanity defense has been presented, the jury must be instructed that it may not consider whether the defendant has met his burden of proving that he is not guilty by reason of insanity until and unless it has first determined that the State has proven the defendant guilty beyond a reasonable doubt of the offense with which he is charged.

720 ILCS 5/6-4 Affirmative Defense

A defense based upon any of the provisions of Article 6 is an affirmative defense except that mental illness is not an affirmative defense, but an alternative plea or finding that may be accepted, under appropriate evidence, when the affirmative defense of insanity is raised or the plea of guilty but mentally ill is made.

C. Case

In the following case, the amended Illinois insanity defense statute in effect at the time of defendant's trial was subsequently found to be unconstitutional. Since the defendant's insanity plea was rejected by the jury, an appeal was filed to address the issue of which statute should have been applied. In reaching its decision, the Illinois Supreme Court discusses the impact the amendments have had on the defense of insanity in this State.

PEOPLE v. RAMSEY
192 Ill.2d 154, 248 Ill.Dec. 882, 735 N.E.2d 533

[Case citations omitted.]

Chief Justice HARRISON delivered the opinion of the court.

BACKGROUND

Following a jury trial in the Circuit Court of Hancock County, defendant, Daniel Ramsey, was convicted of two counts of first degree murder, three counts of attempted first degree murder, and one count each of aggravated criminal sexual assault, home invasion and residential burglary. In finding defendant guilty of these offenses, the jury rejected defendant's claim that he was insane under section 6-2 of the Criminal Code of 1961, as amended by section 15 of Public Act 89-404. On appeal, defendant argues that the amended version of the insanity defense statute was unconstitutional and should not have been followed. Defendant contends he should have been tried under the former version of the law with its broader definition of insanity and its less stringent burden of proof. For the reasons that follow, we reverse defendant's convictions and remand for a new trial.

At issue in this appeal is the law governing defendant's insanity defense. The trial proceedings utilized the version of the insanity defense statute as amended by section 15 of Public Act 89-404 because that was the version of the law in effect when the crimes were allegedly committed. The amended version of the law was significant because it altered the definition of insanity. Under the amendment, a defendant could no longer raise an insanity defense based on his inability "to conform his conduct to the requirements of law." In addition, the amendment increased a defendant's burden of proof for an insanity defense from "a preponderance of the evidence" to "clear and convincing evidence."

***

ANALYSIS

While defendant's appeal was pending, this court held in another case that Public Act 89-404 is unconstitutional in its entirety. As a result, the law is void; it is as though no such law had ever been passed. Section 6-2 of the Criminal Code therefore remained as it was before the adoption of Public Act 89-404's amendments, and those amendments should not have been applied at defendant's trial.

CONCLUSION

The judgment of the Circuit Court must therefore be reversed and the cause remanded for a new trial in accordance with the version of the law in effect prior to Public Act 89-404. In reaching this conclusion, we note that the General Assembly has now enacted new legislation containing the same revisions to the insanity defense statute originally included in Public Act 89-404. The new legislation, set forth in Public Act 90-593, section 15, is not claimed to suffer from the same... problems that rendered Public Act 89-404 invalid, and we must presume it to be constitutional. The new law, however, cannot be applied on retrial....[the new law] would violate the prohibition against *ex post facto* laws....

***

For the foregoing reasons, defendant's convictions and sentences are reversed, and this cause is remanded for a new trial. On retrial, defendant shall be allowed to assert an insanity defense in accordance with section 6-2 of the Criminal Code as it existed prior to the amendments contained in Public Acts 89-404 and 90-593. Specifically, defendant shall be allowed to present an insanity defense based on his inability to conform his conduct to the law. In addition, he shall only be required to prove his insanity at the time of the offense by a preponderance of the evidence.

D. Critical Thinking

► At trial, the State always has the burden of proving the elements of the offense *beyond a reasonable doubt.* Under the former insanity defense statute, the defendant had to establish he was not guilty by reason of insanity by a *preponderance of the evidence.* How does the standard of "clear and convincing" evidence compare to these other standards?

II. Entrapment

A. Comments

Entrapment is an affirmative defense available to the individual who commits a crime because he or she was induced to do so by a government actor or agent. The law on entrapment was developed by courts primarily during the first half of the twentieth century. The Illinois legislature subsequently adopted a statutory definition of the defense. The statute on entrapment, which appears below, was amended in 1996. While the previous statute required the prosecution to establish that the criminal purpose originated with the defendant, the amendment lessened that burden. Presently, the State can meet its burden by proving the defendant was predisposed to commit such a crime. The significance of this change in the law is explained in the case which follows.

B. Statute

720 ILCS 5/7-12 Entrapment

A person is not guilty of an offense if his or her conduct is incited or induced by a public officer or employee, or agent of either, for the purpose of obtaining evidence for the prosecution of that person. However, this Section is inapplicable if the person was pre-disposed to commit the offense and the public officer or employee, or agent of either, merely affords to that person the opportunity or facility for committing an offense.

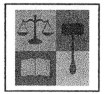

C. Case

When reading the case below, pay particular attention to the significance the court attaches to the change in the entrapment statute from "criminal purpose which the defendant originated" to the current language "if he was predisposed to commit the offense." This case is also a good example of how the *ex post facto* clauses of the Illinois and the U.S. Constitutions allow individuals to rely on the meaning of legislation in effect at the time of the alleged offense, and are to be given fair warning of any changes.

PEOPLE v. CRISS
307 Ill.App.3d 888, 241 Ill.Dec. 647, 719 N.E.2d 776 (1 Dist. 1999)

[Case citations omitted.]

Justice ZWICK delivered the opinion of the court.

BACKGROUND

Defendant, Erin Criss, was charged by indictment with one count of delivery of a controlled substance. Defendant was tried by a jury and presented the defense of entrapment. The jury rejected this defense and found defendant guilty of the charged offense. Defendant was sentenced to a term of nine years' imprisonment. On appeal, defendant seeks reversal or a new trial and raises several issues, among them: (1) whether the trial court erred in instructing the jury regarding the affirmative defense of entrapment, and (2) whether defendant was proved guilty beyond a reasonable doubt.

On January 7, 1993, the defendant sold cocaine to an undercover officer (UC) with the Drug Enforcement Administration (DEA). The UC had been introduced to the defendant by a confidential informant (CI), who lived in defendant's apartment building. The record reflects that defendant was charged by indictment with delivery of more than 100 grams, but less than 400 grams, of cocaine.

At the jury instruction conference following presentation of the evidence at trial, defense counsel requested that the jury receive the version of the Illinois Pattern Jury Instructions (IPI) on entrapment which existed at the time the offense was committed, rather than the amended version existing at the time of trial. The trial court refused this request and issued the current version of the entrapment instruction. The jury found defendant guilty, and the court imposed a sentence of nine years' imprisonment. On appeal, defendant asserts that the prosecution failed to present sufficient evidence to rebut evidence of the affirmative defense of entrapment.

ANALYSIS

Here, the jury heard evidence that originally the transaction was to take place in defendant's apartment, but she informed Martin that they could not consummate the deal there because someone was in her apartment. Defendant then indicated that the sale would have to occur in [the CI's] apartment. Defendant suggested that she collect the money, count it, and then take it upstairs to her apartment before bringing the drugs down to [the CI's] apartment. When [the UC] objected to this plan, defendant readily agreed to bring a portion of the drugs downstairs from her apartment, collect $1,000 and then bring down more narcotics and collect more money. The transaction occurred in this manner, with defendant leaving [the CI's] apartment three different times and returning again with narcotics each time.

In addition, defendant offered to have the last portion, which consisted of a large chunk, broken up. Defendant also gave [the UC] some additional papers and her business card, on which she had written her pager number. Defendant and [the UC] then devised a plan by which [the UC] could use a certain code to page defendant so that defendant would know that it was [the UC] calling. When [the UC] complained that the purchase price was too high, defendant reassured her that it would be different later because the supplier would owe them. This evidence supports the argument that defendant was in control of the situation and directed the transaction. As such, the jury could have concluded that [the CI] merely afforded defendant the opportunity to commit the offense which originated with the defendant. Based upon the foregoing, we hold that the jury could have found defendant guilty beyond a reasonable doubt.

[D]efendant asserts that the trial court should have granted her request that the jury receive the version of the entrapment instruction which existed at the time the offense was committed.

The jury instruction on entrapment which existed in 1993 provided as follows:

"It is a defense to the charge made against the defendant that he was entrapped, that is, that for the purpose of obtaining evidence against the defendant, he was incited or induced by a [a public employee and/or agent of a public employee] to commit an offense.
However, the defendant was not entrapped if [a public employee and/or agent of a public employee] merely afforded to the defendant the opportunity or facility for committing an offense in furtherance of a *criminal purpose which the defendant originated.*" (Emphasis added.)

The language of this pattern jury instruction mirrored that of the entrapment statute which was in effect at the time of the offense. However, the legislature subsequently enacted Public Act 89-332, which amended the entrapment statute, and the IPI instruction was revised to conform to the statutory amendment. Accordingly, when defendant was tried for delivery of a controlled substance, the IPI instruction on entrapment provided as follows:

"It is a defense to the charge made against the defendant that he was entrapped, that is that for the purpose of obtaining evidence against the defendant, he was incited or induced by [a public employee and/or agent of a public employee] to commit an offense.

However, the defendant was not entrapped *if he was predisposed to commit the offense* and [a public employee and/or agent of a public employee] merely afforded to the defendant the opportunity or facility for committing an offense." (Emphasis added.)

Defendant argues that the issuance of the newer amended jury instruction was improper because it misstated the applicable law at the time of the offense and caused her to be convicted under an *ex post facto* law. We agree.***

Illinois courts have long recognized the essential nature of the defendant's predisposition in a case where the affirmative defense of entrapment has been raised. However, prior to the amendment of the entrapment statute, the State was required to prove more than mere predisposition on the part of the defendant to defeat this defense. Before 1996, the critical inquiry in an entrapment case was whether the "criminal purpose" *originated* with the defendant. The amendment of the entrapment statute eliminated the need for the prosecution to prove that defendant had originated the criminal purpose. Instead, the State need only establish that the defendant was predisposed to commit the offense.

Although there is a logical link between the two concepts, having a predisposition to commit an offense is *not* synonymous with having originated a criminal purpose. We think it obvious that every person who originates a criminal purpose is predisposed to commit the offense. Thus, proof that the defendant originated the criminal purpose simultaneously establishes that the defendant was predisposed to commit the crime. However, the reverse is not true. It cannot be said that a person who is predisposed to commit an offense will necessarily be the one who originated its criminal purpose. Consequently, proof of predisposition is insufficient to satisfy the State's burden of proving origination of the criminal purpose.

Generally, predisposition is established by proof that the defendant was ready and willing to commit the crime without persuasion and before his or her initial exposure to government agents. Factors commonly considered include: (1) the defendant's initial reluctance or ready willingness to commit the crime; (2) the defendant's familiarity with drugs and willingness to accommodate the needs of drug users; (3) the defendant's willingness to make a profit from the illegal act; (4) the defendant's prior or current use of illegal drugs; (5) the defendant's participation in testing or cutting the drugs; (6) the defendant's engagement in a course of conduct involving similar offenses; (7) the defendant's ready access to a drug supply; and (8) the defendant's subsequent activities.

Significantly, the evidence which is relevant to establish predisposition goes beyond the temporal circumstances of the charged offense, and the defendant's conduct before and after the alleged offense are relevant. In addition, each of the above factors involves only the defendant and his actions.***

CONCLUSION

As the law existed in 1993, the State could not meet its burden of proof by merely establishing a predisposition by the defendant. Rather, the State was obligated to prove that the defendant had actually originated the criminal purpose. The amendment of the statute in 1996 and the revision of the corresponding pattern jury instruction dramatically altered the burden on the State in rebutting evidence of entrapment. We hold that this amendment constituted a material change in the law by lessening the prosecution's burden in overcoming evidence of entrapment. As such, it operated to deprive defendant of a defense which was available at the time she was alleged to have committed the offense. Because the amended version of the statute and jury instruction became effective almost three years after the alleged offense, defendant was entitled to have the jury instructed on the law as it existed in January 1993. Accordingly, defendant's conviction is vacated, and the cause is remanded for a new trial.

***

D. Web Activity

Keith Jacobson was indicted for violating a provision of the Child Protection Act of 1984 for his purchase of two Bare Boys magazines containing photographs of nude preteen and teenage boys. At his jury trial, Jacobson pleaded entrapment. Jacobson was convicted and the Court of Appeals affirmed his conviction. The case, *Jacobson v. U.S.*, was heard by the U.S. Supreme Court. Find the case at the URL below and answer the following question:

http://caselaw.lp.findlaw.com/scripts/getcase.pl?navby=case&court=us&vol=503&page=540

► What does the U.S. Supreme Court in the majority opinion say about Jacobson's predisposition to commit the offense for which he was convicted?

► How does the analysis of the U.S. Supreme Court in the *Jacobson* case compare with the analysis of the Illinois Appellate Court in the *Criss* case?

III. Compulsion

A. Comment

The defense of compulsion, or duress, has long been recognized in Illinois as an excuse for behavior which appears to fall within the definition of an offense. The basis for the defense is that the individual was compelled to act as he did because of a threat of imminent death or serious harm to himself; otherwise, he would not have performed such an act. Compulsion is an affirmative defense which the State must disprove. The defendant assumes the burden of introducing sufficient evidence of compulsion for the factfinder to have a reasonable doubt as to guilt.

The individual must reasonably believe he is facing imminent death or serious harm, although the belief may be mistaken. A threat of future injury is insufficient. The statute envisions the type of fear that serves to deprive the individual of his or her free will. Compulsion is available as long as it is not the fault of the person using it as a defense. Compulsion is not available to a charge of murder. Nor is the defense available to one who has the opportunity to withdraw from the act but does not.

Subsection (b) simply clarifies that an excuse for the commission of a crime based on the marital relation recognized under common law is not recognized in Illinois.

B. Statute

720 ILCS 5/7-11 Compulsion

(a) A person is not guilty of an offense, other than an offense punishable with death, by reason of conduct which he performs under the compulsion of threat or menace of the imminent infliction of death or great bodily harm, if he reasonably believes death or great bodily harm will be inflicted upon him if he does not perform such conduct.

(b) A married woman is not entitled, by reason of the presence of her husband, to any presumption of compulsion, or to any defense of compulsion except that stated in Subsection (a).

C. Case

In the following case, the defendant, Debra Roberson, did not dispute that her actions violated the Illinois statute regarding leaving the scene of an accident. The issue for the jury was whether defendant had a legal excuse. On appeal, Roberson alleges her public defender should have presented a defense of compulsion rather than a defense of necessity. In deciding the case, the appellate court examines the differences between the two defenses. Roberson may have considered that traditionally, the coercive power forming the basis of a necessity defense comes from the forces of nature, and for a defense of compulsion, the coercive power comes from a human. Here, the court determined the defense of compulsion was not available.

PEOPLE v. ROBERSON
269 Ill.Dec. 420, 780 N.E.2d 1144 (4 Dist. 2002)

[Case citations omitted.]

Justice McCULLOUGH delivered the opinion of the court:

BACKGROUND

The defendant, Debra L. Roberson, was found guilty of leaving the scene of an accident. The accident occurred on April 29, 2001, at or near the intersection of Williamsburg and Summit Ridge in Champaign. Defendant was driving her Chevrolet Malibu. The operator of the other vehicle, a 1989 Chevrolet Blazer, was Terrence Avant. There was a small dent in the Blazer, while defendant's car was ore extensively damaged. The defendant did not stop; remain at the scene; and give her name, address, registration number, driver's license number, and identity of the owner of the vehicle.

Defendant's friend, Charika Williams, was a passenger in Avant's vehicle. Avant was Williams's boyfriend. Defendant testified that she was upset with Williams when she saw Williams in Avant's truck. She wanted to talk to Williams, and she tapped on the window of the vehicle and yelled at Williams to get out of the truck. According to defendant, Avant threw the truck into park, jumped out, grabbed her, threw her to the ground, and proceeded to hit and kick her. She was swinging and kicking to get him off her. After Avant drove away, she followed because she was upset and wanted to talk to Williams. Avant made a U-turn, and she turned right behind him. That was when the collision occurred. She did not stop after the collision because she was afraid that Avant was going to hit her, and she decided to find them later. When she drove away, Avant chased her for 5 or 10 minutes. She was proceeding to Avant's mother's house when she was stopped by the police. She thought Avant would not hurt her at his mother's house and after having time to cool off. On appeal, defendant alleges, *inter alia*, that her attorney provided ineffective assistance by failing to present a defense of compulsion rather than a defense of necessity.

ANALYSIS

The defenses of compulsion and necessity are defined by statute. Unless the State's evidence raises the issue, the defendant must present some evidence on the defense to raise the issue. A defendant is entitled to have a jury instructed on a legally recognized defense that has some foundation in evidence.

Compulsion is a defense distinct from necessity. Compulsion implies complete deprivation of free will and the absence of choice; necessity involves choice between two or more admitted evils. Under the necessity defense, conduct that would otherwise be an offense is justified if the defendant was (1) without blame in occasioning or developing the situation and (2) reasonably believed the conduct was necessary to avoid a public or private injury greater than the injury that might reasonably result from her own conduct. By contrast, the defense of compulsion provides that, except for an offense punishable with death, a person is not guilty of an offense if (1) she performs the conduct under the compulsion of threat or imminent infliction of death or great bodily harm and (2) she reasonably believed death or great bodily harm would be inflicted on her if she did not perform such conduct. The defense of compulsion generally requires an impending imminent threat of great bodily harm together with a demand that the person perform a specific criminal act for which he is eventually charged.

CONCLUSION

There was no evidence in this case that Avant, or anyone else, threatened defendant with imminent infliction of death or great bodily harm unless she left the scene of the accident. In this case, although defendant testified she was concerned that Avant would be threatening or cause her harm if she stopped, that behavior by Avant never occurred. Defendant was not compelled to leave the scene of the accident. In addition, the evidence shows defendant followed Avant and the collision occurred because of defendant's conduct.

***

D. Critical Thinking

▶ Considering the circumstances and the fact that defendant and Avant knew one another, do you believe it was necessary for defendant to remain at the scene?

▶ If you had been a passenger in the defendant's car, what action would you have recommended she take and still be in compliance with the law?

IV. Mistake and Intoxication

A. Comment

There are numerous laws in Illinois of which we may not be specifically aware. Regardless, we accept the fact that ignorance of the law is no defense. The Illinois statute accepts the general rule that a mistake as to a matter of law or fact which negates a mental state that is an element of the offense charged will serve as a defense. Subsection (b) lists situations under which the defense may be raised. Subsection (c) provides for the situation where a defendant, because of ignorance or mistake, may not be convicted of a particular offense, but may be found guilty of another, included offense which does not require the same mental state.

Note also that a person may claim a defense by virtue of being in an intoxicated or drugged state only if that condition was created involuntarily. Further, the defendant must establish the condition deprived him of substantial capacity either to appreciate that his conduct was illegal or to conform his conduct to the law. While it may be easier to conjure up a situation where an individual may be slipped a mind-altering drug, involuntary intoxication may occur as a result of trickery, fraud or deceit. Voluntary intoxication is no longer accepted as a defense in Illinois.

B. Statutes

720 ILCS 5/4-8 Ignorance or mistake

(a) A person's ignorance or mistake as to a matter of either fact or law, except as provided in Section 4-3(c) [720 ILCS 5/4-3 Mental State], is a defense if it negatives the existence of the mental state which the statute prescribes with respect to an element of the offense.

(b) A person's reasonable belief that his conduct does not constitute an offense is a defense if:

(1) The offense is defined by an administrative regulation or order which is not known to him and has not been published or otherwise made reasonably available to him, and he could not have acquired such knowledge by the exercise of due diligence pursuant to facts known to him; or

(2) He acts in reliance upon a statute which later is determined to be invalid; or

(3) He acts in reliance upon an order or opinion of an Illinois Appellate or Supreme Court, or a United States appellate court later overruled or reversed;

(4) He acts in reliance upon an official interpretation of the statute, regulation or order defining the offense, made by a public officer or agency legally authorized to interpret such statute.

(c) Although a person's ignorance or mistake of fact or law, or reasonable belief, described in this Section 4-8 is a defense to the offense charged, he may be convicted of an included offense of which he would be guilty if the fact or law were as he believed it to be.

(d) A defense based upon this Section 4-8 is an affirmative defense.

720 ILCS 5/6-3 Intoxicated or drugged condition

A person who is in an intoxicated or drugged condition is criminally responsible for his conduct unless such condition is involuntarily produced and deprives him of substantial capacity either to appreciate the criminality of his conduct or to conform his conduct to the requirements of law.

C. Questions

Please choose the correct answer for the following questions.

1. For a successful defense, the defendant must establish he was not guilty by reason of insanity by which standard?

a. preponderance of the evidence
b. clear and convincing evidence
c. beyond a reasonable doubt
d. beyond a shadow of a doubt

2. In order for a jury to reach a verdict of guilty but mentally ill, they must find the defendant:

a. was sane at the time the crime was committed
b. is sane at the time of trial
c. was not criminally responsible for his conduct
d. has presented an actual defense

3. To defeat the affirmative defense of entrapment, the prosecutor must prove:

a. the defendant has previously been convicted of a similar offense
b. the criminal purpose originated with the defendant
c. the defendant was predisposed to commit the offense
d. all of the above

4. Which of the following statements is true regarding the defense of compulsion:

a. compulsion is an affirmative defense
b. defendant must have acted under the threat of imminent infliction of death or great bodily harm
c. the defense of compulsion does not apply to a charge of murder
d. all of the above

5. A defendant who was in an intoxicated or drugged condition at the time of the offense:

a. is always criminally responsible for his conduct
b. may have a defense if the intoxication was voluntary
c. may have a defense if the intoxication was involuntary
d. none of the above

CHAPTER NINE

Offenses Directed Against the Person: Homicide

I. First Degree Murder

A. Comment

Homicide is the killing of one person by another. Under certain circumstances, a homicide may be justifiable or excusable. On the other hand, murder is always a criminal offense. First-degree murder is the most serious crime brought before the courts. Consequently, a defendant convicted of first-degree murder in Illinois may receive the death penalty.

The first-degree murder statute set forth below contains three subsections describing the different forms of the crime of murder. The subsections define the requisite mental state or act for each form. Keep in mind, that there is only one crime of murder, not three separate offenses.

In addition to the homicide statutes contained in this chapter, Illinois also has laws addressing homicide of an unborn child, concealment of homicidal death, and drug-induced homicide.

B. Statute

720 ILCS 5/9-1 First degree Murder...

(a) A person who kills an individual without lawful justification commits first degree murder if, in performing the acts which cause the death:
(1) he either intends to kill or do great bodily harm to that individual or another, or knows that such acts will cause death to that individual or another; or
(2) he knows that such acts create a strong probability of death or great bodily harm to that individual or another; or
(3) he is attempting or committing a forcible felony other than second degree murder.

***

C. Case

In the *Reed* case, defendant was charged with two different forms of first-degree murder for the killing of a 23-month-old boy. Defendant testified that he never intended to hurt the boy. Following conviction on both counts, defendant appealed. Note the Appellate Court's analysis regarding the requisite mental state for first-degree murder. Also note how the court addresses multiple convictions for a single act of murder.

PEOPLE v. REED
298 Ill.App.3d 285, 232 Ill.Dec. 529, 698 N.E.2d 620 (1 Dist. 1998),
appeal denied, 181 Ill.2d 585, 235 Ill.Dec. 946, 706 N.E.2d 501 (1998)

[Case citations omitted.]

Justice O'BRIEN delivered the opinion of the court:

BACKGROUND

Crystal Thomas met the defendant, 18-year-old Keith Reed, in May 1992 and they became boyfriend and girlfriend. Crystal had a 21-month-old son, Kevin, by a previous relationship. She and Kevin sometimes spent the night with defendant at his house in Chicago.

On July 20, 1992, Crystal and Kevin went to defendant's house, where they spent the next five days. On July 21 and July 22, 1992, Crystal noticed some injuries to Kevin, specifically, a discoloration of his eye and a little cut on the side of his lip. She asked defendant about the cause of Kevin's injuries, and defendant responded that the cut lip was from a "rug burn" and the discolored eye resulted from some bacteria or dust.

On July 24, 1992, Crystal and defendant had an argument concerning the frequent phone calls from Kevin's father. Defendant wanted the phone calls to stop, and he wanted to know whether Crystal intended to get back together with Kevin's father. During the argument, defendant knocked over some items that were sitting on the dining room table, punched and broke a fan, and swung a trophy around.

The following morning, July 25, 1992, Crystal got ready to run some errands. Before leaving around 9 a.m., she checked on Kevin who was sleeping in only a diaper. She did not notice anything wrong with him. Crystal returned to the house around 3 p.m. and was met there by defendant's brother, who told her that Kevin was at the hospital. Crystal went to the hospital where she was told that her baby was in surgery. A policeman then took her to the station where she was questioned and was told that Kevin was dead.

Having received a call, detectives met with defendant at the hospital. The defendant told detectives that Crystal left his house around 9:30 that morning, leaving defendant alone with Kevin. Defendant stated Kevin woke up around noon, and defendant went to change his diaper. At that time, defendant noticed that Kevin was having trouble walking. Defendant noticed that Kevin's eyes did not look right and that he appeared "spacey." Defendant stated he did not know how Kevin suffered the injuries that caused his death.

The autopsy showed extensive bruising on Kevin's head, chest, abdomen, arms, and legs. There was also a large area of hemorrhage beneath the scalp on the right and left side of the head. There were 14 internal injuries in the chest and abdominal cavity. The doctor stated Kevin's internal injuries happened only hours before his death.

When re-interviewed by detectives, defendant admitted to tossing Kevin in the air, and back handing him on the chest a couple of times. Defendant called his brother who came over and said the baby did not look right. That is when defendant called the paramedics. Defendant said he never intended to hurt Kevin at any time.

Following a bench trial, defendant was convicted of two counts of first-degree murder and sentenced to 60 years' imprisonment. On appeal, defendant contends, *inter alia*, the State failed to prove him guilty beyond a reasonable doubt.

ANALYSIS

Defendant argues the State failed to prove he acted with any of the mental states specified in the murder statute. Defendant argues the evidence showed he acted recklessly and asks us to reduce his conviction to involuntary manslaughter.

Defendant here was charged with the forms of murder defined in sections 9-1(a)(1) and (a)(2) of the Criminal Code of 1961. The statute states:
A person who kills an individual without lawful justification commits first degree murder if, in performing the acts which cause the death:
(1) he either intends to kill or do great bodily harm to that individual or another, or knows that such acts will cause death to that individual or another; or
(2) he knows that such acts create a strong probability of death or great bodily harm to that individual or another.

Defendant argues that the evidence failed to establish that he intended to kill or cause Kevin great bodily harm, or that he knew his acts would cause death or would create a strong probability of death or great bodily harm to Kevin. We disagree.

The requisite mental state may be inferred from defendant's conduct and the circumstances surrounding his commission of the crime. Disparity in size and strength between the defendant and the victim and the nature and extent of the victim's injuries are relevant circumstances in ascertaining whether the defendant possessed the necessary mental state.

Here, defendant was an 18-year-old male, about 6 feet tall and 180 pounds. The victim, Kevin, was a 23-month-old baby, 33.4 inches in length and weighing 28.4 pounds. The evidence established that Kevin died of multiple injuries due to blunt trauma, and the injuries were of a type seen in an automobile accident or in a child who had fallen out of a third-story window. Given the disparity in size between defendant and Kevin, the extent of Kevin's injuries and the force needed to cause them, we conclude that the trial judge could infer that defendant acted with the necessary mental state to support a conviction for first-degree murder.

CONCLUSION

We also note that the evidence established that the injuries were inflicted at a time when Kevin was home alone with defendant. Further, defendant admitted striking Kevin. Taking the evidence in the light most favorable to the prosecution, any rational trier of fact could find defendant guilty of murder beyond a reasonable doubt.

We also address defendant's argument that we must vacate one of his murder convictions. Defendant was charged with and convicted of murder under sections 9-1(a)(1) and (a)(2) of the Code. However, defendant cannot be convicted of more than one murder arising out of the same physical act. When multiple murder convictions have been entered for the same act, the less culpable conviction must be vacated. A murder conviction under section 9-1(a)(2) involves a less culpable mental state than a conviction under section 9-1(a)(1). Therefore, we affirm defendant's conviction under section 9-1(a)(1) and vacate defendant's conviction under section 9-1(a)(2).

***

D. Critical Thinking

► What facts did the appellate court consider in determining that the trial judge could have inferred defendant acted with the required mental state for first-degree murder?

► Why did the prosecutor charge the defendant with two counts of first-degree murder when there was only one victim?

II. Felony Murder

A. Comment

Section (a)(3) of the first-degree murder statute defines the form of murder commonly referred to as felony murder. The felony murder rule applies equally to all participants involved in the felony even if the death of the victim was unintended. The reasoning behind the felony murder doctrine is that an individual who intends to commit a forcible felony should also be held criminally liable for the foreseeable results of his actions which occur during the commission of the original felony.

B. Case

The following case is a good example of the application of the felony murder rule where the death was unintended. The intended victim of an armed robbery fired the fatal shot which killed an innocent bystander. The Illinois Supreme Court held that the felony murder doctrine applied because the retaliation of the shooter was a reasonably foreseeable event.

PEOPLE v. LOWERY
178 Ill.2d 462, 227 Ill.Dec. 491, 687 N.E.2d 973 (1997)

[Case citations omitted.]

Chief Justice FREEMAN delivered the opinion of the court:

BACKGROUND

On March 20, 1993, defendant, Antonio Lowery, was arrested and charged with two counts of armed robbery and one count of attempt armed robbery of Maurice Moore, Marlon Moore, and Robert Thomas. Defendant was also charged with the murder of Norma Sargent. In his statement to the police, defendant explained that he and his companion, "Capone," planned to rob Maurice, Marlon, and Robert. As Maurice, Marlon, and Robert walked along Leland Avenue in Chicago, defendant approached them, pulled out a gun and forced Maurice into an alley. Capone remained on the sidewalk with Robert and Marlon. Once in the alley, defendant demanded Maurice's money. Maurice grabbed defendant's gun and a struggle ensued. Meanwhile, Capone fled with Robert in pursuit. Marlon ran into the alley and began hitting defendant with his fists. As defendant struggled with Maurice and Marlon, the gun discharged. The three continued to struggle onto Leland Avenue. Upon pushing Maurice down, defendant noticed that Maurice now

114

had the gun. Defendant then ran from the place of the struggle to the corner of Leland and Magnolia Avenues, where he saw two women walking. As he ran, he heard gunshots and one of the women scream. One of the women was fatally shot.

Defendant continued to run, and in an apparent attempt at disguise, he turned the Bulls jacket which he was wearing inside-out. He was subsequently apprehended by the police and transported to the scene of the shooting, where Maurice identified him as the man who had tried to rob him.

The jury found defendant guilty of first-degree murder under the felony-murder doctrine, two counts of armed robbery, and one count of attempted armed robbery. The appellate court reversed, holding that there was insufficient evidence to sustain a conviction for felony murder and remanded the cause for resentencing on defendant's armed robbery and attempted armed robbery convictions.

ANALYSIS

At issue in this appeal is whether the felony-murder rule applies where the intended victim of an underlying felony, as opposed to the defendant or his accomplice, fired the fatal shot which killed an innocent bystander. To answer this question, it is necessary to discuss the theories of liability upon which a felony-murder conviction may be based. The two theories of liability are proximate cause and agency.

In considering the applicability of the felony-murder rule where the murder is committed by someone resisting the felony, Illinois follows the "proximate cause theory." Under this theory, liability attaches under the felony-murder rule for any death proximately resulting from the unlawful activity—notwithstanding the fact that the killing was by one resisting the crime.

Alternatively, the majority of jurisdictions employ an agency theory of liability. Under this theory, "the doctrine of felony murder does not extend to a killing, although growing out of the commission of the felony, if directly attributable to the act of one other than the defendant or those associated with him in the unlawful enterprise." Thus, under the agency theory, the felony-murder rule is inapplicable where the killing is done by one resisting the felony.

It is consistent with reason and sound public policy to hold that when a felon's attempt to commit a forcible felony sets in motion a chain of events which were, or should have been, within his contemplation when the motion was initiated, he should be held responsible for any death which by direct and almost inevitable sequence results from the initial criminal act. Thus, there is no reason why the principle underlying the doctrine of proximate cause should not apply to criminal cases. Moreover, we believe that the intent behind the felony-murder doctrine would be thwarted if we did not hold felons responsible for the foreseeable consequences of their actions.

***

Based on the plain language of the felony-murder statute, legislative intent, and public policy, we decline to abandon the proximate cause theory of the felony-murder doctrine....

Because we have decided to adhere to the proximate cause theory of the felony-murder rule, we must now decide whether the victim's death in this case was a direct and foreseeable consequence of defendant's armed and attempted armed robberies.***a felon is liable for those deaths which occur during a felony and which are the foreseeable consequence of his initial criminal acts.

In the present case, when defendant dropped the gun and realized that Marlon [sic] was then in possession of the weapon, he believed that Marlon would retaliate, and, therefore, he ran. If decedent's death resulted from Marlon's firing the gun as defendant attempted to flee, it was, nonetheless, defendant's action that set in motion the events leading to the victim's death. It is unimportant that defendant did not anticipate the precise sequence of events that followed his robbery attempt. We conclude that defendant's unlawful acts precipitated those events, and he is responsible for the consequences.

***

[Defendant contends] that Marlon was not legally justified in firing at defendant....There is no claim that Marlon shot at defendant in self-defense or in an attempt to arrest him. Moreover, the proper focus of this inquiry is not whether Marlon was justified in his actions, but whether defendant's actions set in motion a chain of events that ultimately caused the death of decedent. We hold that defendant's actions were the proximate cause of decedent's death and the issue of whether Marlon's conduct was justified is not before this court.

CONCLUSION

...[W]e hold that the evidence was sufficient to prove defendant guilty beyond a reasonable doubt under the felony-murder rule....We therefore reverse the appellate court.***Accordingly, we remand the cause to the appellate court for consideration of defendant's remaining issues.

C. Critical Thinking

► In planning the robbery, do you believe Lowery actually thought about the possibility of Marlon getting control of Lowery's gun, firing it, striking and killing an innocent bystander?

► Do you think it is reasonable for the law to hold a felon liable for a death under the "proximate cause theory?"

III. Second Degree Murder

A. Comment

Although the Illinois General Assembly abolished the offense of voluntary manslaughter and created the offense of second-degree murder, the elements of second-degree murder are the same as those for the former offense of voluntary manslaughter. The change applied to homicides which occurred after December 31, 1986. The current statute points out that a person commits the offense of second-degree murder when he commits the offense of first-degree murder but there exists one of two mitigating factors outlined in the statute. If the prosecutor proves the elements of first-degree murder beyond a reasonable doubt, the defendant then has the burden of establishing the existence of a mitigating factor by a preponderance of the evidence. If the defendant establishes one of the mitigating factors, the factfinder will then have the option of finding the defendant guilty of second-degree murder.

For the factfinder to consider a conviction of second-degree murder there must exist either serious provocation, or the defendant's unreasonable belief that his use of deadly force was necessary to prevent imminent death or great bodily harm. The presence of either mitigating factor can reduce first-degree murder to second-degree murder. The mental state for first-degree murder and second-degree murder are the same; either intent or knowledge.

B. Statute

720 ILCS 5/9-2 Second Degree Murder

(a) A person commits the offense of second degree murder when he commits the offense of first degree murder as defined in paragraphs (1) or (2) of subsection (a) of Section 9-1 of this Code [720 ILCS 5/9-1 First Degree Murder] and either of the following mitigating factors are present:
(1) At the time of the killing he is acting under a sudden and intense passion resulting from serious provocation by the individual killed or another whom the offender endeavors to kill, but he negligently or accidentally causes the death of the individual killed; or
(2) At the time of the killing he believes the circumstances to be such that, if they existed, would justify or exonerate the killing under the principles stated in Article 7 of this Code [720 ILCS 5/7-1 et seq. Justifiable Use of Force], but his belief is unreasonable.
(b) Serious provocation is conduct sufficient to excite an intense passion in a reasonable person.

(c) When a defendant is on trial for first degree murder and evidence of either of the mitigating factors defined in subsection (a) of this Section has been presented, the burden of proof is on the defendant to prove either mitigating factor by a preponderance of the evidence before the defendant can be found guilty of second degree murder. However, the burden of proof remains on the State to prove beyond a reasonable doubt each of the elements of first degree murder and, when appropriately raised, the absence of circumstances at the time of the killing that would justify or exonerate the killing under the principles stated in Article 7 of this Code [720 ILCS 5/7-1 et seq.]. In a jury trial for first degree murder in which evidence of either of the mitigating factors defined in subsection (a) of this Section has been presented and the defendant has requested that the jury be given the option of finding the defendant guilty of second degree murder, the jury must be instructed that it may not consider whether the defendant has met his burden of proof with regard to second degree murder until and unless it has first determined that the State has proven beyond a reasonable doubt each of the elements of first degree murder.

(d) Sentence. Second Degree Murder is a Class 1 felony.

C. Case

Although there is an extensive procedural history involved in this case, the court's decision below addresses the issue of whether the jury should have been instructed on the offense of second-degree murder. The defendant, Richard Nitz, was convicted of first-degree murder for the killing of Michael Miley. The evidence showed the victim, a homosexual, followed defendant to his trailer, exited his car, and approached the front steps of defendant's front porch. The evidence further showed that defendant struck the victim with a baseball bat, shot him in the head and mutilated his body. The appellate court discusses the appropriateness of a second-degree murder instruction.

PEOPLE v. NITZ
319 Ill.App.3d 949, 254 Ill.Dec. 281, 747 N.E.2d 38, (5 Dist. 2001)

[Case citations omitted.]

Justice KUEHN delivered the opinion of the court:

BACKGROUND

Nitz [appeals] the trial judge's refusal to instruct on the offense of second-degree murder. Nitz argues that the second-degree murder instruction was warranted on the basis of mutual quarrel or combat. The instruction should be given where there exists some evidence of serious provocation which if believed by the jury, would reduce the crime to second-degree murder.

A person commits second-degree murder when "[a]t the time of the killing he is acting under a sudden and intense passion resulting from serious provocation by the individual killed or another whom the offender endeavors to kill, but he negligently or accidentally causes the death of the individual killed." "Serious provocation: is defined as 'conduct sufficient to excite an intense passion in a reasonable person'." The defendant must be acting under a sudden and intense passion spurred from serious provocation that the law recognizes as reasonable. The only categories of provocation that courts recognize as sufficient to warrant a second-degree-murder instruction are mutual quarrel or combat, substantial physical injury or assault, illegal arrest, or adultery with one's spouse. Passion on behalf of the defendant, no matter how violent, will not relieve him of culpability for first-degree murder unless it is engendered by provocation that the law recognizes as reasonable.

Mutual quarrel or combat is defined as a "fight or struggle entered into by both parties willingly or by mutual fight upon a sudden quarrel and in hot blood upon equal terms***." In addition, the evidence will not support a second-degree-murder instruction where there is provocation but the defendant's retaliation is not proportional.

We find that the trial court did not abuse its discretion in refusing to give Nitz's second-degree-murder instruction, because Nitz did not present sufficient evidence to warrant giving that instruction. There is nothing in the evidence to establish that Nitz was acting under a sudden and intense passion resulting from serious provocation at the time he beat and killed Miley. This was not "mutual combat or quarrel" as that term has been defined. It was not a fight on equal terms.

In an attempt to support his claim of mutual quarrel or combat, Nitz points to testimony that Miley followed him to his trailer, exited his car, and advanced to the steps of Nitz's front porch. Nitz also points to the testimony…that Nitz [said] he had killed a homosexual with whom he had a "run-in," and the testimony…that Nitz had [said] words had been exchanged before Nitz killed Miley.

Mere words, gestures, or trespass to property do not constitute the kind of serious provocation contemplated by the statute. The evidence here shows that there was no struggle with Miley prior to the time that Nitz struck him with a baseball bat, shot him in the head, and decapitated him. The evidence shows that no more than words were exchanged. No evidence was presented to show that Miley threatened Nitz, and even if the victim's act of following Nitz home could be viewed as provocation, Nitz's retaliation was not proportional. The nature of the contact characterized by Nitz beating Miley with a baseball bat while Miley remained "unarmed" could hardly meet the definition of mutual combat, which envisions a fight or struggle on equal terms.

CONCLUSION

Accordingly, under the facts of this case, no second-degree-murder instruction was warranted, and the trial court did not abuse its discretion by rejecting that instruction.

D. Critical Thinking

▶ The appellate court points out that even in situations involving serious provocation the law requires that any retaliation be proportional. What does that mean? Why has the law imposed such a requirement?

IV. Involuntary Manslaughter and Reckless Homicide

A. Comment

The offenses of involuntary manslaughter and reckless homicide are defined in the same statute. The elements which must be proved by the prosecution are the same for both offenses except that the prosecution must show the defendant charged with reckless homicide was driving a motor vehicle at the time the crime occurred. To obtain a conviction, the state must establish beyond a reasonable doubt that: (1) the defendant performed an act which caused the death of another; (2) the act was performed in such a way that it was likely to cause death or great bodily harm; and (3) such act was performed recklessly.

The primary difference between these offenses and murder is the mental state which accompanies the act causing the death of another human being. Recklessness is the required intent for involuntary manslaughter and reckless homicide; the killing need not be deliberate.

It is important to note that Illinois now has a statute addressing the involuntary manslaughter of a family or household member. It is a separate offense and is defined in 725 ILCS 5/5112A-3. For conviction, the prosecution must prove beyond a reasonable doubt the elements of involuntary manslaughter plus the element that the victim was a family or household member. The penalty is a Class 2 felony.

B. Statute

720 ILCS 5/9-3 Involuntary Manslaughter and Reckless Homicide

(a) A person who unintentionally kills an individual without lawful justification commits involuntary manslaughter if his acts whether lawful or unlawful which cause the death are such as are likely to cause death or great bodily harm to some individual, and he performs them recklessly, except in cases in which the cause of the death consists of the driving of a motor vehicle or operating a snowmobile, all-terrain vehicle, or watercraft, in which case the person commits reckless homicide.

(b) In cases involving reckless homicide, being under the influence of alcohol or any other drug or drugs at the time of the alleged violation shall be presumed to be evidence of a reckless act unless disproved by evidence to the contrary.

(c) For the purposes of this Section, a person shall be considered to be under the influence of alcohol or other drugs while:

1. The alcohol concentration in the person's blood or breath is 0.08 or more based on the definition of blood and breath units in Section 11-501.2 of the Illinois Vehicle Code [625 ILCS 5/11-501.2 Chemical and other tests];

2. Under the influence of alcohol to a degree that renders the person incapable of safely driving a motor vehicle or operating a snowmobile, all-terrain vehicle, or watercraft;

3. Under the influence of any other drug or combination of drugs to a degree that renders the person incapable of safely driving a motor vehicle or operating a snowmobile, all-terrain vehicle, or watercraft; or

4. Under the combined influence of alcohol and any other drug or drugs to a degree which renders the person incapable of safely driving a motor vehicle or operating a snowmobile, all-terrain vehicle, or watercraft.

(d) Sentence.

(1) Involuntary manslaughter is a Class 3 felony.

(2) Reckless homicide is a Class 3 felony.

(e) [Exceptions listed.]

(f) In cases involving involuntary manslaughter in which the victim was a family or household member as defined in paragraph (3) of Section 112A-3 of the Code of Criminal Procedure of 1963 [725 ILCS 5/112A-3], the penalty shall be a Class 2 felony, for which a person if sentenced to a term of imprisonment, shall be sentenced to a term of not less than 3 years and not more than 14 years.

C. Cases

The defendant, Bernard Burnette, was charged with first-degree murder. The judge, however, found Burnette guilty of involuntary manslaughter based on the evidence presented at trial. On appeal, the defendant challenged the involuntary manslaughter conviction. The appellate court found the state had, in fact, failed to prove the defendant guilty beyond a reasonable doubt and vacated Burnette's involuntary manslaughter conviction.

PEOPLE v. BURNETTE
325 Ill.App.3D 792, 259 Ill.Dec. 268, 758 N.E.2d 391 (1 Dist. 2001),
rehearing denied, appeal denied, 198 Ill.2d 597, 262 Ill.Dec. 621, 766 N.E.2d 241

[Case citations omitted.]

Presiding Justice COHEN delivered the opinion of the court:

BACKGROUND

Defendant, Bernard Burnette, was charged by indictment with multiple counts of first-degree murder, home invasion, armed violence and residential burglary. After a bench trial, Burnette was convicted of one county of involuntary manslaughter and one count of home invasion and was sentenced to concurrent prison terms of 5 and 20 years, respectively. On appeal, Burnette challenges both the sufficiency of the evidence supporting his convictions as well as the basis of his sentence. We affirm in part and vacate in part.

Burnette's apartment in Chicago had been burglarized twice, on February 13 and March 18, 1996. Shortly after the first burglary, Burnette purchased a .38-caliber handgun and ammunition on the street for $50, "to use as protection." Burnette testified that on March 19, 1996, he had a telephone conversation with ex-girlfriend Latrice Grant, during which Grant confessed to him that she had burglarized his apartment. She also told him that he could retrieve his property the following weekend at her apartment, which Burnette knew Grant now shared with Michael Wells.

Burnette testified that on March 24, 1996, after first attempting to contact Grant by telephone, Burnette went to her apartment to collect his property. Burnette testified that his gun was in the pocket of the "Starter" jacket he wore to the apartment. Burnette denied that he had intentionally taken the gun to the apartment, stating that since he purchased the gun, he had carried it on a continuing basis for personal protection. Upon arriving at the apartment, Burnette climbed the five steps to the porch and knocked on the back door. Wells answered the door, allowing Burnette into the kitchen. Wells went to notify Grant of Burnette's arrival. Wells returned shortly, telling Burnette that Grant was busy and that Burnette should return later. As he made his way out the door, Burnette asked Wells to tell Grant that he would be returning later that evening. As Burnette exited the back door, Wells closed the door on the fingers of Burnette's hand, causing pain but no injury. The two men then engaged in name calling. Wells followed Burnette out onto the porch and struck him on the back of the neck with his fist.

A fight then ensued on the back porch. As the two men fought, they ended up in the kitchen crashing into cabinets and appliances. Wells threatened to kill Burnette. During their struggle in the kitchen, Burnette's gun fell from his pocket to the kitchen floor, spinning to rest approximately three feet from the back door. Wells dove for the gun. Just as Wells grasped the gun, Burnette kicked Wells' arm, causing the gun to fall to the floor a second time. Both men then went to their knees and took hold of opposite ends of the gun. The gun went off. Burnette retrieved the gun and ran from the apartment and discarded the gun. Burnette denied that he had intended to shoot Wells.

The trial court found Burnette not guilty of first-degree murder, apparently accepting Burnette's assertion that he had killed Wells unintentionally during a struggle. The court rejected Burnette's self-defense claim. The court did, however, find Burnette guilty of involuntary manslaughter predicated on Burnette's recklessness in bringing a gun to a potentially dangerous confrontation. According to the trial court, "the victim would not have been murdered by a handgun if Mr. Burnette had not brought that handgun to the scene."

ANALYSIS

The crux of involuntary manslaughter is recklessness. A person is reckless or acts recklessly, when he consciously disregards a substantial and unjustifiable risk that circumstances exist or that a result will follow, described by the statute defining the offense; and such disregard constitutes a gross deviation from the standard of care which a reasonable person would exercise in the situation. Thus, for purposes of involuntary manslaughter, a person acts recklessly when he consciously disregards a substantial and unjustifiable risk that his acts are likely to cause death or great bodily harm to another.

We believe that the trial court misconstrued the involuntary manslaughter statute in predicating Burnette's conviction solely on his recklessness in bringing the gun to Wells' apartment. The question here is one of proximate cause. Wells died not because Burnette brought the gun to his apartment, but because he was *shot* when the gun discharged during the struggle in the kitchen. This is not a case in which a defendant deliberately drew a handgun and brought it into play during a fight, or deliberately pointed a loaded gun at another while intoxicated.

Based on the evidence credited by the trial court, the gun fell from Burnette's pocket in the kitchen during his struggle with Wells. Wells reached the gun first, but Burnette kicked it from his hand. Both men then dove for the gun, reaching it at the same time. When asked why he then reached for the gun, Burnette replied, "I was afraid [Wells] might shoot me with it. He was talking about he was going to 'kill me....'" In convicting Burnette of involuntary manslaughter, the trial court accepted Burnette's statement that the firing of the gun was unintentional. Logically, then, the killing must have been the result of either recklessness or accident.

CONCLUSION

After a careful review of the record, we hold that the trial judge's subsequent determination that Wells died as the result of recklessness is contrary to the manifest weight of the evidence. Burnette's recklessness in bringing the gun to the apartment was too attenuated with respect to the shooting itself, the "act which cause[d] the death," to support an involuntary manslaughter conviction. The State failed to prove beyond a reasonable doubt that Burnette was reckless at the time of the shooting. Burnette's conviction on the charge of involuntary manslaughter is therefore vacated.

***

PEOPLE v. BECK
295 Ill.App.3d 1050, 230 Ill.Dec. 419, 693 N.E.2d 987 (2 Dist. 1998),
appeal denied, 179 Ill.2d 592, 235 Ill.Dec. 568, 705 N.E.2d 441 (1998)

[Case citations omitted.]

Justice THOMAS delivered the opinion of the court:

BACKGROUND

On the evening of November 26, 1994, Sandra Meadows was driving her Lincoln Towncar southbound on Route 251 in rural Ogle County, Illinois. Her daughter, Shawna Meadows, was in the front passenger seat, and her mother, Alleta Priest, was in the rear passenger seat. At that same time, the defendant, Paul C. Beck, was driving his Ford van northbound on Route 251. The two vehicles collided, injuring Sandra and defendant and killing Shawna and Alleta.

Evidence presented at trial included the results of a doctor-ordered test revealing defendant had a blood alcohol level of .1392 grams per 100 liters following the collision. Testimonial evidence established that defendant crossed over the center line and into the southbound lane of traffic prior to impact.

The jury found defendant guilty of two counts of reckless homicide for which he was sentenced to concurrent 10-year prison terms. The defendant appealed his convictions.

ANALYSIS

This court has recognized that a defendant is guilty of reckless homicide when the State proves beyond a reasonable doubt that (1) he was operating a motor vehicle; (2) he unintentionally caused a death while operating the vehicle; and (3) the acts which caused the death were performed recklessly so as to create a likelihood of death or great bodily harm to some person. Intoxication is not an element of reckless homicide; however, evidence of intoxication is probative on the issue of recklessness. If the State introduces evidence of intoxication in a reckless homicide case, it need only present some evidence of intoxication from which, along with other circumstances, recklessness may be inferred. Whether recklessness has been proved is an issue to be decided by the trier of fact.

...[W]e find that the evidence presented in this case was sufficient to support defendant's reckless homicide convictions. The record unequivocally establishes that defendant was operating a motor vehicle and that he unintentionally caused the deaths of Shawna Meadows and Alleta Priest. The record also establishes that defendant acted recklessly in causing their deaths.

The State introduced ample evidence of defendant's intoxication, which was probative on the issue of recklessness....Despite this evidence of recklessness, defendant argues that the deaths were caused by his van's mechanical failure. We find defendant's argument to be without merit. Although there was evidence that defendant had had problems starting the van on the day of the accident and that the headlights had gone out prior to the collision, defendant testified that he had no difficulty with the van's steering. Unlike defendant's intoxicated condition, the mechanical problems with the van did not provide a rational explanation for the van's being in the oncoming lane of traffic at the time of the collision.

CONCLUSION

We conclude that the evidence...was sufficient to support a jury finding beyond a reasonable doubt that defendant committed reckless homicide resulting in the deaths....Thus, we affirm defendant's convictions of reckless homicide.

E. Critical Thinking

► In the *Burnette* case, the appellate court pointed out the trial judge was required to find Burnette reckless at the time of the shooting, in other words, "the act which caused death," in order to convict on involuntary manslaughter. Do you think the trial judge was confused about how to interpret the law? Do you think the trial judge allowed his personal feelings regarding gun ownership to influence his ruling?

► In the *Beck* case, the appellate court stated that intoxication is not an element of reckless homicide. What did the court mean when it stated "evidence of intoxication is probative on the issue of recklessness?"

V. Death Penalty in Illinois

A. Comment

In January 2000, former Illinois Governor, George H. Ryan ordered a moratorium on executions due to the number of wrongful convictions in this State. Shortly before leaving office, Ryan removed all 171 prison inmates from Illinois' death row. In November 2003, the General Assembly passed legislation containing reforms to the state's death penalty procedures. The moratorium on executions continues under Governor Rod Blagojevich. The Governor's Commission on Capital Punishment continues to make recommendations to improve the system. Despite the moratorium, the prosecution may still seek the death penalty in appropriate cases.

For updated information on the status of the death penalty in Illinois, and for links and resources, visit:

URL: http://www.deathpenaltyinfo.org/article.php?scid=6&did=483#recent

URL: http://www.law.northwestern.edu/wrongfulconvictions/

B. Questions

Please choose the correct answer for the following questions.

1. The mental state of either intent or knowledge is required for conviction on the charge of:

a. first-degree murder only
b. first-degree or second-degree murder
c. second-degree murder and involuntary manslaughter
d. reckless homicide

2. The killing of an individual while committing a forcible felony is commonly known as:

a. second-degree murder
b. involuntary manslaughter
c. felony murder
d. justifiable homicide

3. The mental state of recklessness is required for conviction on the charge of:

a. reckless homicide only
b. reckless homicide or involuntary manslaughter
c. felony murder
d. voluntary manslaughter

4. "Serious provocation" and "unreasonable belief in justification" are mitigating factors which may reduce a charge of first-degree murder to:

a. felony murder
b. second-degree murder
c. involuntary manslaughter
d. reckless homicide

5. The prosecution must show a specific intent to kill for a conviction of:

a. felony murder
b. involuntary manslaughter
c. reckless homicide
d. none of the above

CHAPTER TEN

Offenses Directed Against the Person:
Kidnapping, Sex Crimes, and Others

I. Kidnapping

A. Comment

The Illinois statute defining the crime of kidnapping has seen little change over the years. Generally, the elements which make up the crime consist of: (1) an unlawful seizure, and (2) secret confinement. At common law, kidnapping required that the victim be removed from the country. Former Illinois law required the victim be transported out of state. Of the three methods of kidnapping outlined in subsection (a) of the current statute, two of the three methods address the movement of the victim from one place to another, although there is no geographical limitation. The mental state element for all three methods of kidnapping is that the defendant acted "knowingly." Subsection (b) s to eliminates the defense that a child under the age of 13 consented to the confinement.

The offense of aggravated kidnapping is defined in a separate statute and is found at 720 ILCS 5/10-2. This offense consists of the elements which make up the crime of kidnapping plus one of the eight elements enumerated in the statute. Aggravated kidnapping addresses situations such as: kidnap for ransom; while armed with a firearm or dangerous weapon; inflicting great bodily harm; or kidnap of a child. Aggravated kidnapping is a Class X felony. A person convicted of a second or subsequent offense shall be sentenced to a term of natural life imprisonment.

B. Statute

720 ILCS 5/10-1 Kidnapping

(a) Kidnapping occurs when a person knowingly:
(1) And secretly confines another against his will, or
(2) By force or threat of imminent force carries another from one place to another with intent secretly to confine him against his will, or
(3) By deceit or enticement induces another to go from one place to another with intent secretly to confine him against his will.
(b) Confinement of a child under the age of 13 years is against his will within the meaning of this section if such confinement is without the consent of his parent or legal guardian.
(c) Sentence. Kidnapping is a Class 2 felony.

C. Case

The defendant, Orrin Dressler, was convicted of several felony offenses including kidnapping and aggravated kidnapping. One of defendant's appeal issues involves his conviction for aggravated kidnapping based upon his act of kidnap while armed with a dangerous weapon. The defendant contends a canister of Mace is not a dangerous weapon for purposes of the aggravated kidnapping statute. The appellate court agreed.

PEOPLE v. DRESSLER
317 Ill.App.3d 379, 250 Ill.Dec. 867, 729 N.E.2d 630 (3 Dist. 2000)

[Case citations omitted.]

Justice LYTTON delivered the opinion of the court:

BACKGROUND

A jury found defendant Orrin Dressler guilty of robbery, armed robbery, kidnapping, aggravated kidnapping with a canister of Mace, aggravated stalking and theft. The jury found defendant not guilty of aggravated kidnapping with a gun. The judge imposed consecutive sentences of 14 and 11 years for armed robbery and aggravated kidnapping, respectively, and concurrent 5-year sentences for aggravated stalking and theft to run concurrently with the longer sentences. No sentences were imposed for robbery and kidnapping.

Mary Jo Senese, a Cook County Sheriff's Deputy, obtained an order of protection against defendant during divorce proceedings that commenced in June of 1995. Around 6:45 a.m. on February 23, 1996, as Senese was about to enter her car for work, a man whom she did not recognize grabbed her, sprayed Mace in her face and forced her into a vehicle. During the ensuing struggle, Senese pulled a wig off the man and recognized the defendant. Defendant handcuffed Senese's hands behind her and removed her service revolver. Defendant then drove her to his house in Lemont, where he handcuffed and chained her to the wall in a small, cement-block room in the basement.

After defendant left the house, Senese worked one handcuff loose and broke another. She proceeded upstairs and called 9-1-1. Senese left the house through the bathroom window before the police arrived and ran to a business on the adjoining property. Senese entered the business around 11:45 a.m. with handcuffs on both wrists and a heavy chain hanging from one of the cuffs. The store manager summoned help. Later that day, defendant was arrested.

Defendant argued on appeal that his conviction for aggravated kidnapping cannot stand because a canister of Mace is not a "dangerous weapon" as contemplated by the statute defining the offense.

ANALYSIS

Section 10-2(a)(5) of the Criminal Code of 1961 states that "[a] kidnapper***is guilty of the offense of aggravated kidnapping when he***[c]ommits the offense of kidnapping while armed with a dangerous weapon....Section 33A-1 defines "dangerous weapons" as those objects that fall within any one of three categories. Category I weapons are firearms—handguns, sawed-off shotguns, sawed-off rifles, other firearms small enough to be concealed upon a person, semiautomatic firearms and machine guns. Category II weapons are other firearms, knives, daggers, dirks, switchblades, stilettos, axes, hatchets or "other deadly or dangerous weapon[s] or instrument[s] of like character." Category III weapons are bludgeons, black-jacks, slung shots, sand-bags, sand-clubs, metal knuckles, billies, "or other dangerous weapon[s] of like character."

CONCLUSION

A canister of Mace cannot arguably fit into any of the foregoing categories of dangerous weapons. It does not fire penetrating projectiles (Category I); it cannot be used to cut the victim (Category II); and it cannot be used to enhance a beating (Category III). Therefore, though noxious sprays may be "dangerous weapons" for purposes of armed robbery, they do not qualify as such for purposes of aggravated kidnapping. Armed robbery does not [define] the definition of dangerous weapons contained in section 33A-1. Defendant's conviction for aggravated kidnapping based on the use of Mace must be vacated.

We affirm defendant's convictions for armed robbery, kidnapping and aggravated stalking; we vacate defendant's convictions and sentences for aggravated kidnapping and theft; we vacate defendant's conviction for robbery. Since we have vacated defendant's aggravated kidnapping conviction and affirmed his kidnapping conviction, we remand the cause for sentencing on the kidnapping conviction.

***

D. Critical Thinking

▶The judge sentenced Dressler to 11 years imprisonment for the aggravated kidnapping. What is the maximum sentence the judge can now impose for the kidnapping conviction? Should the judge consider the defendant's use of Mace as an aggravating factor justifying imposition of the maximum sentence for the kidnapping conviction?

▶Since the sentence for aggravated kidnapping was to run consecutive to the 14 year sentence for armed robbery, how did the appellate court's decision change the amount of time defendant is to serve in prison?

E. Web Activity

Information regarding the status of individuals imprisoned or on parole may be accessed on the Illinois Department of Corrections website. To view information on Orrin Dressler, for example, visit:

URL: http://www.idoc.state.il.us/subsections/search/default.asp

▶using the "Last Name" search method, enter "Dressler"
▶click on "Inmate Search"

II. Criminal Sexual Assault

A. Comment

While the term "rape" may be used in a generic sense in Illinois today, the actual "Rape" statute, along with several other statutes defining sex offenses, was replaced some years ago by the Criminal Sexual Assault Act. The Criminal Sexual Assault Act created the new offenses of criminal sexual assault, aggravated criminal sexual assault, criminal sexual abuse, and aggravated criminal sexual abuse. This comprehensive Act was adopted to alleviate the need for multiple statutes proscribing various sex acts and to cover gender gaps which previously existed under the law.

The intent of the revised statutes under the Criminal Sexual Assault Act was to increase the number of convictions for sex-related offenses. The statutory terms are now broader and the focus is on the acts of the offender rather than the state of mind of the victim. For offenses involving "sexual penetration," where no specific mental state is identified, a mental state of "intent, knowledge or recklessness" is implied. Where use of force is an element of the offense, there is no absolute standard defining the amount of force required.

Conduct which constituted rape under the former statute, i.e., forcible sexual penetration, is now included in the Criminal Sexual Assault statute in subsection (a). The former rape law applied only to a male offender, at least 14 years of age, and a female victim, not his wife, by force and against her will. The current statute is broader in that it covers criminal other acts of sexual penetration under specific circumstances.

The offense of Aggravated Criminal Sexual Assault is defined in 720 ILCS 5/12-14. This crime consists of the act of criminal sexual assault plus the presence of one of the many aggravating factors listed in the statute. Generally, the aggravating factors cover situations where: a firearm or other dangerous weapon was used; there was bodily harm done to the victim; or the victim was of a certain age or suffered from some disability. Aggravated Criminal Sexual Assault is a Class X felony. A second or subsequent offense carries a term of natural life in prison.

The Criminal Sexual Abuse statute covers unlawful sexual conduct not involving forcible sexual penetration. The requisite mental state for this offense is knowledge of the act and intent to arouse. Medical evidence of the crime is not required for conviction. Depending upon the conduct of the defendant, criminal sexual abuse may be either a misdemeanor or a felony.

The offense of Aggravated Criminal Sexual Abuse is defined in 720 ILCS 5/12-16. The crime consists of the act of criminal sexual abuse plus the presence of one of several aggravating factors listed in the statute. The aggravating factors are similar to those listed in the Aggravated Criminal Sexual Assault statute. Aggravated Sexual Abuse is a Class 2 felony.

B. Statutes

720 ILCS 5/12-12 Definitions

...(e) "Sexual conduct" means any intentional or knowing touching or fondling by the victim or the accused, either directly or through clothing, of the sex organs, anus or breast of the victim or the accused, or any part of the body of a child under 13 years of age, or any transfer or transmission of semen by the accused upon any part of the clothed or unclothed body of the victim, for the purpose of sexual gratification or arousal of the victim or the accused.

(f) "Sexual penetration" means any contact, however slight, between the sex organ or anus of one person by an object, the sex organ, mouth or anus of another person, or any intrusion, however slight, of any part of the body of one person or of any animal or object into the sex organ or anus of another person, including but not limited to cunnilingus, fellatio or anal penetration. Evidence of emission of semen is not required to prove sexual penetration.

***

720 ILCS 5/12-13 Criminal Sexual Assault

(a) The accused commits criminal sexual assault if he or she:
(1) commits an act of sexual penetration by the use of force or threat of force; or
(2) commits an act of sexual penetration and the accused knew that the victim was unable to understand the nature of the act or was unable to give knowing consent; or
(3) commits an act of sexual penetration with a victim who was under 18 years of age when the act was committed and the accused was a family member; or

(4) commits an act of sexual penetration with a victim who was at least 13 years of age but under 18 years of age when the act was committed and the accused was 17 years of age or over and held a position of trust, authority or supervision in relation to the victim.

(b) Sentence.

(1) Criminal sexual assault is a Class 1 felony.

***

720 ILCS 5/12-15 Criminal sexual abuse

(a) The accused commits criminal sexual abuse if he or she:

(1) commits an act of sexual conduct by the use of force or threat of force; or

(2) commits an act of sexual conduct and the accused knew that the victim was unable to understand the nature of the act or was unable to give knowing consent.

(b) The accused commits criminal sexual abuse if the accused was under 17 years of age and commits an act of sexual penetration or sexual conduct with a victim who was at least 9 years of age but under 17 years of age when the act was committed.

(c) The accused commits criminal sexual abuse if he or she commits an act of sexual penetration or sexual conduct with a victim who was at least 13 years of age but under 17 years of age and the accused was less than 5 years older than the victim.

(d) Sentence. Criminal sexual abuse for a violation of subsection (b) or (c) of this Section is a Class A misdemeanor. Criminal sexual abuse for a violation of paragraph (1) or (2) of subsection (a) of this Section is a Class 4 felony.

***

C. Case

Brad Lieberman had been convicted of several rapes in 1980. Just days before Lieberman was to be released from prison in 2000, the State filed a petition alleging that Lieberman fit the definition of a "sexually violent person" and was, therefore, subject to involuntary civil commitment to the Department of Human Services. Lieberman filed a motion to dismiss the State's petition. Part of Lieberman's argument was that subsequent to his convictions, the Illinois legislature abolished the crime of rape, and that "rape" was not listed as a "sexually violent offense" for purposes of commitment. In order to address this issue, the Illinois Supreme Court began its analysis with a discussion on the history of, and the reasons for, the repeal of the rape statute and the adoption of the current Criminal Sexual Assault Act. Part of that discussion appears in the case below.

In re DETENTION OF BRAD LIEBERMAN
(The People of the State of Illinois, Appellant, v. Brad Lieberman, Appellee).

201 Ill.2d 300, 267 Ill.Dec. 81, 776 N.E.2d 218,
rehearing denied, certiorari denied 2003 WL 138693.

[Case citations omitted.]

Justice MC MORROW delivered the opinion of the court:

BACKGROUND

In 1980, Lieberman was convicted in the Circuit Court of Cook County of six counts of rape and one count of attempted rape. That same year, Lieberman was found guilty of one count of rape and one count of attempted rape in Lake County. Lieberman was sentenced to a number of terms of imprisonment to run concurrently, the longest of which required him to serve 40 years in prison.

Lieberman was scheduled to be released from the Illinois Department of Corrections on January 9, 2000. On January 6, 2000, the State filed in the Circuit Court of Cook County a petition pursuant to section 15 of the Commitment Act alleging that respondent is a "sexually violent person" within the meaning of the Act and therefore subject to involuntary civil commitment to the control, care and custody of the Department of Human Services. In support of this petition, the State alleged that in 1980 Lieberman was convicted of multiple "sexually violent offenses." The petition further alleged that Lieberman suffered from several mental disorders, including paraphilia and "sexually attracted to non-consenting females, non-exclusive type." The petition also alleged that Lieberman was subject to involuntary civil commitment under the Act because he was "dangerous to others" and that "his mental disorders create a substantial probability that he will engage in future acts of sexual violence." Lieberman filed a motion to dismiss noting that the crime of rape was abolished by the General Assembly in 1984 as part of a comprehensive rewriting of this state's sex offense statutes. Lieberman further observed that, under the Act in effect at the time the State filed the petition at bar, a "sexually violent offense" for purposes of the Act [did not include the offense of "rape."]

***

ANALYSIS

We are asked in this appeal to determine whether a conviction for the crime of rape constitutes a "sexually violent offense" within the meaning of the version of the Sexually Violent Persons Commitment Act in effect at the time the State filed its petition in the Circuit Court. ***

The Sexually Violent Persons Commitment Act took effect on January 1, 1998. The Act applies to an individual who has been convicted of a "sexually violent offense" and who is nearing release or discharge from custody. The Act allows the State to petition the court for the civil detention of criminal offenders beyond their imposed periods of incarceration if the State can show that the offender satisfies the criteria of a "sexually violent person."

In order to determine whether individuals, such as Lieberman, who were convicted of the now-repealed offense of rape are subject to civil commitment under the version of the Commitment Act in effect at the time the State filed the petition at bar, we must first address the threshold question of whether the former offense of rape was subsumed into the subsequently enacted crimes of criminal and aggravated criminal sexual assault. In answering this question, we must discern the legislature's intent in repealing the offense of rape and enacting a new statutory scheme governing the prosecution of sex crimes.

In 1984, the General Assembly enacted Public Act 83-1067, more commonly known as the Criminal Sexual Assault Act. The Act repealed eight statutes which had defined sex offenses...of the Criminal Code of 1961, including the offense of rape. This court has previously observed that the Criminal Sexual Assault Act recodified the sexual offenses into a comprehensive statute with uniform statutory elements that would criminalize all sexual assaults without distinguishing between the sex of the offender or the victim and the type of sexual act proscribed. To this end, the Criminal Sexual Assault Act replaced the repealed offenses with the newly created offenses of criminal sexual assault, aggravated criminal sexual assault, criminal sexual abuse, and aggravated criminal sexual abuse.***

In contrast to the offense of rape, which could be charged only where the offender was male and the victim was female, the subsequently enacted offenses of criminal and aggravated criminal sexual assault use gender-neutral language, thereby widening the range of these offenses. In addition, although the offense of rape focused on the victim's state of mind and required a showing by the prosecutor that the crime was committed against the victim's will, the offenses of criminal and aggravated criminal sexual assault to not require evidence of the state of mind of the victim. Furthermore, an individual may charge his or her spouse with the offenses of criminal and aggravated criminal sexual assault, whereas the offense of rape could only be committed by a male against a female who was not his wife. Finally, the Criminal Sexual Assault Act also broadened several of the definitions relating to sexual crimes. For example, the definition of "penetration" under the repealed rape statute was limited to the penetration of the female sex organ by the male sex organ. In contrast, the subsequently enacted criminal sexual assault statute defines "penetration" far more broadly as "any contact, however slight," and "any intrusion, however slight."

135

The above comparisons reveal that the conduct underlying Lieberman's rape convictions would have also subjected respondent to charges under the subsequently enacted criminal sexual assault statutes. ...[T]he legislature, acknowledging that rape encompasses all types of sexual assault, redrafted the sex crimes law in order to create a comprehensive statute which recognizes several gradations of conduct traditionally considered "rape." The legislative debates show that the redrafting of these laws was intended to address the reality that the Illinois sex crimes statutes, had, over time, become overly cumbersome, unduly restrictive, and archaic, that a wholesale revision was necessary to "create statutes which reflected information learned in past decades about the nature of sexual assault," and that the revised statutes were intended to increase the number of sex-crime convictions. To this end, not only have the subsequently enacted sex offenses been framed in terms broader than those found in the former offense of rape, the new offenses are also defined in terms of the behavior of the offender rather than the state of mind of the victim.

CONCLUSION

We conclude that in creating the offenses of criminal and aggravated criminal sexual assault, the General Assembly intended that the elements of the former offense of rape be subsumed into these new offenses.

***

D. Critical Thinking

▶ The Illinois Supreme Court points out several differences between the former crime of rape and the criminal sexual assault statute we have today. How do these changes further the goal of the legislature to increase convictions of sex offenders?

III. Crimes Against Children

A. Comment

Children are among the most vulnerable in our society as potential crime victims. Perpetrators may target a victim whom they believe lacks strength to resist an assault, or credibility should the crime be reported. Illinois law is replete with statutes addressing the special concerns of children.

The former Illinois statutes of indecent liberties with a child and sexual contact with an individual under the age of 16 were repealed and replaced under the Criminal Sexual Assault Act discussed above.

B. Case

Robert Calusinski was convicted of criminal sexual abuse. The trial judge found there was sufficient evidence of "sexual conduct" where the defendant placed his tongue in the mouth of a six-year-old while kissing her. This case demonstrates how sexual conduct may be implied from the circumstances.

PEOPLE v. CALUSINSKI

314 Ill.App.3d 955, 247 Ill.Dec. 956, 733 N.E.2d 420 (2 Dist. 2000)

[Case citations omitted.]

Justice GEIGER delivered the opinion of the court:

BACKGROUND

On July 16, 1998, the defendant, Robert Calusinski, was charged by indictment with the offense of criminal sexual abuse. The indictment alleged that, on June 22, 1998, the defendant, by threat or use of force, committed an act of sexual conduct with the six-year-old victim, J.R. Specifically, the defendant was alleged to have placed his tongue in the victim's mouth for the purpose of his sexual arousal. The indictment also alleged that the defendant had previously been convicted of indecent liberties with a child in 1983.

At trial, the victim testified that she was six years old. She testified that, a couple of days after her birthday, she went outside to look for a stuffed animal that she had lost in her yard. When she went outside, she took a flashlight because it was dark. The victim saw the defendant standing in her front yard. The victim's mother had testified that when the little girl came back into the house, she had a "shocked" look on her face. The victim stated that the defendant had grabbed her, kissed her, and put his tongue in her mouth. The mother called the health department and the police department.

During an interview with law enforcement, the defendant stated that he had kissed the victim on the cheek on the day in question because it was her birthday. The defendant also stated that it was possible that his mustache may have touched the corner of the victim's mouth during the kiss. The defendant denied putting his tongue in the victim's mouth but said that his tongue may have touched her cheek. The defendant said that the victim's mouth was closed during the kiss.

The trial court found the defendant guilty of criminal sexual abuse. In making its findings, the trial court commented that it had found the victim's testimony compelling and credible. The trial court noted that the victim's testimony at trial was consistent with the statement she had made to her mother immediately following the incident. The trial court also noted the defendant's statements to the police acknowledging that he kissed the victim and that his tongue might have touched her cheek.

The defendant was sentenced to seven years' imprisonment. One of the defendant's issues on appeal is that he was not proved guilty beyond a reasonable doubt. The defendant argues that there was no physical evidence that the alleged incident occurred.

ANALYSIS

One commits the offense of criminal sexual abuse if he commits an act of sexual conduct by the use of force or threat of force. For purposes of the offense of criminal sexual abuse, "sexual conduct" is defined as "any intentional or knowing touching or fondling by the victim or the accused, either directly or through clothing, of***any part of the body of a child under 13 years of age for the purpose of sexual gratification or arousal of the victim or the accused." The defendant's sexual gratification or arousal may be inferred from the evidence.

After a careful review of the record, we conclude that the State introduced sufficient evidence to prove the defendant guilty beyond a reasonable doubt. The testimony of the prosecuting witness, even when standing alone, may be sufficient to uphold a defendant's conviction. Although there was no physical evidence that the alleged kiss occurred, the trial court was presented with the victim's own testimony that the defendant had placed his hands on her, kissed her, and put his tongue in her mouth. The trial court had the opportunity to observe the victim's testimony and found it to be credible and convincing. Such a determination is entitled to great weight.

Moreover, we note that the victim's trial testimony substantially corroborated the statement that she made to her mother immediately following the incident. As noted above, the victim told her mother that the defendant had grabbed her, kissed her, and put his tongue in her mouth. Additionally, we also note that, in his statements to the police, the defendant acknowledged that he kissed the victim and that it was possible that his tongue might have touched her cheek. We believe that the evidence, when taken as a whole, was sufficient to establish that the defendant forcefully took hold of the victim and placed his tongue in the victim's mouth.

For purposes of the instant offense, sexual conduct is defined as the intentional or knowing touching or fondling of any part of the body of a child under 13 years of age for the purpose of sexual gratification or arousal of the accused. It has been established that, under the appropriate circumstances, kissing can constitute sexual conduct. The Illinois Supreme Court has noted that kissing often serves as a preliminary stimulant for arousing or appealing to sexual passions and desires.

In the instant case, the defendant placed his tongue in the mouth of a six-year-old girl. Despite the defendant's assertions, we cannot ascribe an innocent motive to such conduct. As noted by the trial court, a "French kiss" is an inherently sexual act which generally results in sexual excitement and arousal.

CONCLUSION

Based on the circumstances, we believe that the trial court could reasonably infer that the defendant intentionally placed his tongue in the victim's mouth for purposes of his own sexual arousal. Therefore, we conclude the defendant committed an act of sexual conduct for purposes of the offense of criminal sexual abuse.

D. Web Activity

In Illinois, convicted sex offenders are required to register with the Department of State Police. To view registration information on Robert Calusinski, for example, visit:

URL: http://www.isp.state.il.us/sor/frames.htm

▶ read and respond to the provisions in the disclaimer;
▶ on the left side of the next screen, click on "search by name;"
▶ enter "Calusinski" and click "submit"

IV. Assault and Battery

A. Comment

At common law, an assault was committed by performing either an act which placed a person in reasonable apprehension of receiving a battery even though the offender did not intend to commit a battery, or by an actual attempt to commit a battery. Former Illinois law defined an assault as "an unlawful attempt", coupled with "a present ability" to perform the act. The statute has since been amended so that proof of an attempted battery, and the intent that goes along with an attempt, is no longer required. The statute simply requires that a person engage in conduct which places another person in reasonable apprehension of receiving a battery. Therefore, assault is not a specific intent crime. The offenses of "assault" and "battery" are distinct violations. An assault does not involve a touching. Any unwanted or otherwise unlawful physical contact of an insulting or provoking nature will constitute a battery.

Aggravated assault is defined in 720 ILCS 5/12-2. The crime consists of the act of assault plus the presence of one of several aggravating factors listed in the statute. There is still no touching involved. Depending upon the conduct of the defendant, aggravated assault may be either a Class A misdemeanor or a Class 4 felony. An assault committed with the use of a firearm, for example, is a felony.

At common law, a battery was committed by any unlawful touching of another. Today, a battery may be committed by either causing bodily harm or by physical contact which is insulting or provoking. An intentional or knowing act performed without legal

139

justification is required. Note that a battery may be committed by "any means." A finger poke to the chest while engaged in an argument, or even spitting in another's face will suffice.

Aggravated battery is defined in 720 ILCS 5/12-4. The crime consists of the act of battery plus the presence of one of many aggravating factors listed in the statute. Generally, aggravated battery may be committed by (1) intentionally or knowingly causing great bodily harm, permanent disability or disfigurement; (2) committing some act which may cause great bodily harm; or (3) causing another to ingest or come into contact with some substance or thing either intended to or likely to cause physical injury or harm. Aggravated battery is a Class 3 or Class 2 felony depending upon the conduct involved.

B. Statutes

720 ILCS 5/12-1 Assault

(a) A person commits an assault when, without lawful authority, he engages in conduct which places another in reasonable apprehension of receiving a battery.
(b) Sentence. Assault is a Class C misdemeanor.

***

720 ILCS 5/12-3 Battery

(a) A person commits battery if he intentionally or knowingly without legal justification and by any means, (1) causes bodily harm to an individual or (2) makes physical contact of an insulting or provoking nature with an individual.
(b) Sentence. Battery is a Class A misdemeanor.

C. Case

On appeal, Daniel Milligan contended the victim's injuries were more consistent with that of a "simple" (misdemeanor) battery rather than aggravated battery, for which he was convicted.

PEOPLE v. MILLIGAN II
327 Ill.App.3d 264, 261 Ill.Dec. 940, 764 N.E.2d 555 (4 Dist. 2002)

[Case citations omitted.]

Presiding Justice MC CULLOUGH delivered the opinion of the court:

BACKGROUND

Following a January 18, 2000, jury trial in the Circuit Court of Ford County, defendant, Daniel Milligan, was convicted of one count of home invasion and one count of aggravated battery. The trial court sentenced defendant to 25 years' imprisonment and 3 years' imprisonment, respectively, the sentences to be served concurrently. On appeal, defendant claims, *inter alia*, that the evidence of great bodily harm to the victim was not sufficient to support the aggravated battery conviction.

The events leading to the charges in this case took place on September 5, 1999. The victim was Melancholy Granger. Defendant and Granger had been drinking and visiting various other people in Ford County. Granger had been driving, and an argument ensued because she did not want defendant to drive after he had been drinking. Granger left defendant at the side of the road and returned home. Defendant later returned to Granger's. As he came running up, she shut and locked her door. Defendant kicked in the front door. He beat Granger with his fists, an answering machine, and a telephone. He struck her in the head, back, and arms; grabbed her throat and choked her; threatened to make her hang herself; and broke a chair over her legs. Granger's parents arrived and called the police. Defendant fled and was later arrested.

Defendant argues that the victim's injuries are insufficient to support the finding of great bodily harm necessary to his aggravated battery conviction. The defendant argues that if the offense of "simple" battery is to have any import at all, the amount of damage necessary for a finding of great bodily harm must be more severe than simple bruises and abrasions.

Whether the victim's injuries rise to the level of great bodily harm is a question for the trier of fact. In making that determination, the relevant inquiry is 'not what the victim did or did not do to treat the injury but what injuries the victim in fact received.'

CONCLUSION

We have examined the photographs of Granger's injuries taken by police and the testimony of the victim's treating physician. The photographs depict Granger with bruises under her eyes, on her back, and on one arm. They also show scratches or cuts on her throat and on one leg. Granger was diagnosed as having multiple contusions, a closed head injury, and leg abrasions. Given the closed head injury and the extent of Granger's abrasions and bruising, we find that the evidence as presented was sufficient to find defendant guilty of aggravated battery beyond a reasonable doubt.

D. Questions

Please choose the correct answer for the following questions.

1. Which of the following is a correct statement of the law in Illinois?

a. The kidnapping statute has been amended several times in the past decade.
b. The mental state for kidnapping is that the defendant acted knowingly.
c. Kidnapping is a misdemeanor offense.
d. Mace is a "dangerous weapon" for purposes of the aggravated kidnapping statute.

2. Which of the following is a correct statement of the law in Illinois?

a. Aggravated criminal sexual assault is a Class 2 felony.
b. For the crime of criminal sexual assault, the focus is on the state of mind of the victim.
c. Criminal sexual assault can be committed by either males or females.
d. Criminal sexual assault requires medical proof of bodily harm.

3. Which of the following is a correct statement of the law in Illinois?

a. Criminal sexual abuse requires proof of forcible sexual penetration.
b. "Sexual conduct" requires skin-to-skin contact.
c. "Sexual conduct" may be established by evidence of touching any part of the body of a child under 13 years of age.
d. Criminal sexual assault is a felony while criminal sexual abuse is only a misdemeanor.

4. Which of the following is a correct statement of the law in Illinois?

a. An assault does not involve a touching.
b. The terms "assault" and "battery" are synonymous.
c. A battery requires a striking or kicking of another against their will.
d. An assault is simply an attempted battery.

5. Which of the following is a correct statement of the law in Illinois?

a. Aggravated battery is a Class X felony.
b. Assault and battery have the same maximum penalty.
c. To be convicted of a battery, the defendant must have caused bodily harm.
d. Aggravated battery may be established by a showing of great bodily harm to the victim.

CHAPTER ELEVEN

Crimes Against Property

I. Theft

A. Comment

A cursory look at Chapter 720, Article 16, of the ILCS reveals a plethora of theft-related offenses. These statutes replace the former offenses of larceny, larceny by trick, embezzlement, and false pretenses, to name a few. Note in the general theft statute the different ways in which the unlawful obtaining of property of another may occur.

Theft is an offense which can be either a misdemeanor or a felony. The distinction depends upon what property is taken, the value of that property, and how the property is taken.

B. Statutes

720 ILCS 6/16-1 Theft

(a) A person commits theft when he knowingly:
(1) Obtains or exerts unauthorized control over property of the owner; or
(2) Obtains by deception control over property of the owner; or
(3) Obtains by threat control over property of the owner; or
(4) Obtains control over stolen property knowing the property to have been stolen or under such circumstances as would reasonably induce him to believe that the property was stolen; or
(5) Obtains or exerts control over property in the custody of any law enforcement agency which is explicitly represented to him by any law enforcement officer or any individual acting in behalf of a law enforcement agency as being stolen, and
(A) Intends to deprive the owner permanently of the use or benefit of the property; or
(B) Knowingly uses, conceals or abandons the property in such manner as to deprive the owner permanently of such use or benefit; or
(C) Uses, conceals, or abandons the property knowing such use, concealment or abandonment probably will deprive the owner permanently of such use or benefit.
(b) Sentence.
(1) Theft of property not from the person and not exceeding $300 in value is a Class A misdemeanor....
(4) Theft of property from the person not exceeding $300 in value, or theft of property exceeding $300 and not exceeding $10,000 in value, is a Class 3 felony....

C. Case

The defendant was found in possession of items stolen from the office of a John Deere dealership. Based upon the defendant's statement to police that he bought the items from someone else, he was charged with, and found guilty of, the section of the theft statute for obtaining control over stolen property. On appeal, the defendant challenged that section of the theft statute as unconstitutionally vague.

PEOPLE v. NELSON
336 Ill.App.3d 517, 271 Ill.Dec. 161, 784 N.E.2d 379 (3 Dist. 2003)

[Case citations omitted.]

Justice LYTTON delivered the opinion of the court:

BACKGROUND

Trevor Hiel worked in his parents' John Deere dealership in Macomb. On August 14, 2000, Trevor went into the dealership office at about 6:15 a.m. He noticed that a laptop computer and a digital camera were missing. The batteries for both items and the battery charger for the camera had not been taken. He saw that the back door was unlocked, and a rear window was broken. After the police came to their office, the Hiels called the store where they had purchased the camera and told the store manager that the camera had been stolen.

On August 15, 2000, the defendant, Delrico J. Nelson, came into the store and asked about how to connect a particular model of digital camera to a computer. The camera he asked about was the same model as the camera stolen from the Hiels' office. The defendant called the store later that morning and ascertained that the store had a battery charger for the same model of camera. The defendant asked if he could bring the battery to the store to make sure it matched the charger. The manager replied that he could and then called the police.

The defendant's girlfriend went to the camera store and purchased a battery charger for the camera at the defendant's request. A police officer made contact with the defendant's girlfriend. She told the officer that the digital camera and laptop computer were at the defendant's residence. Several officers then went to the defendant's home. One officer knocked on the door of the residence while other officers watched the sides and back of the house. After no one answered, an officer saw the defendant come out of the bedroom window and walk between the bushes and the house. The officer took the defendant into custody. A police officer advised the defendant of his *Miranda* rights. He told the defendant that he had spoken to his girlfriend about the stolen laptop and camera. The defendant led him to the room where the items were located.

At the police station, the defendant said that at about 4:00 a.m. on August 14, 2000 he was contacted by Mark Woolam who asked if he wanted to buy a laptop computer and a digital camera. The defendant said he purchased the items for a total of $380. Trevor testified that the value of the camera at the time it was stolen was between $400 and $499, and the value of the computer was about $900. The camera store manager said that the value of the camera was between $350 and $400. An expert testified that the value of the computer was between $900 and $1,100.

The defendant told the officers that Woolam said the items were not stolen. When the defendant asked Woolam for a receipt, Woolam refused, saying that he did not want to put his name on anything.

The defendant was charged with theft by knowingly obtaining control over property under such circumstances as would reasonably induce him to believe that the property was stolen. The jury found the defendant guilty and he was sentenced to five years imprisonment.

ANALYSIS

The defendant argues that the language in section 16-1(a)(4)(A) of the theft statute, prohibiting a person from knowingly obtaining control over stolen property "under such circumstances as would reasonably induce him to believe that the property was stolen," is unconstitutionally vague under the Fourteenth Amendment Due Process Clause....A criminal statute may be vague and, therefore, violate a defendant's due process rights, if it (1) fails to provide the type of notice that would enable a person of ordinary intelligence to understand what conduct is prohibited, or (2) authorizes or encourages arbitrary and discriminatory enforcement by the police. The defendant submits that the statutory language in question is unconstitutional under both prongs of the Supreme Court's test for vagueness.

The defendant contends that the statutory language in question is too vague because it does not give a person of ordinary intelligence sufficient notice of what conduct is prohibited....The defendant was charged under the statute with obtaining possession "under such circumstances as would reasonably induce him to believe that the property was stolen." This language gave the defendant sufficient notice that his conduct was prohibited. Here, Woolam yelled at the defendant on the street at 4 a.m. and then asked if he would be interested in purchasing two electronic items. The defendant purchased the items for $380. The testimony at trial established that the value of these items was at least $1,250. When the defendant asked Woolam for a receipt, Woolam said that he did not want to put his name on anything.

Based on these facts, we believe that a person of ordinary intelligence presented with the computer and camera under these circumstances would reasonably be induced to believe that the merchandise had been stolen....Illinois courts have consistently used an objective test for the *mens rea* element of theft by receiving stolen property.***

CONCLUSION

The language in section 16-1(a)(4)(A) of the Illinois theft statute, "under such circumstances as would reasonably induce him to believe that the property was stolen," is not unconstitutionally void for vagueness.

The judgment of the McDonough County Circuit Court is affirmed.

D. Critical Thinking

► In the Appellate Court's analysis, the value of the stolen items is discussed in relation to the amount the defendant paid for them. For what other reason would the value of the items in this case be important?

► The defendant was convicted of a Class 2 felony. Burglary is also a Class 2 felony. Do you think the defendant's sentence should be the same whether he committed the burglary, or bought the stolen items from the person who did commit the burglary?

II. Computer Crime and Identity Theft

A. Comment

As technology changes, so must the law. Criminals are always thinking up new and innovative means to achieve their illegal goals. Common use of the personal computer has opened up a new world to thieves as well as those who abide by the law. In response to these fraudulent activities, the Illinois legislature has enacted laws specifically addressing computer crime and identity theft. Of the many offenses involving the use of a computer contained in the Criminal Code, computer fraud is included in this section for your review.

According to the Federal Trade Commission, there were 7,474 reports of identity theft in Illinois during 2002. On July 31, 2003, a new identity theft law went into effect replacing the former financial identity theft statute. The new law expands upon, and better defines the actions covered in an effort to better protect the security of personal information. As you review this statute, note the expanded subsection on sentencing.

B. Statutes

720 ILCS 5/16D-5 Computer Fraud

(a) A person commits the offense of computer fraud when he knowingly:

(1) Accesses or causes to be accessed a computer or any part thereof, or a program or data, for the purpose of devising or executing any scheme, artifice to defraud, or as part of a deception;

(2) Obtains use of, damages, or destroys a computer or any part thereof, or alters, deletes, or removes any program or data contained therein, in connection with any scheme, artifice to defraud, or as part of a deception; or

(3) Accesses or causes to be accessed a computer or any part thereof, or a program or data, and obtains money or control over any such money, property, or services of another in connection with any scheme, artifice to defraud, or as part of a deception.

(b) Sentence. (1) A person who commits the offense of computer fraud as set forth in subsection (a)(1) of this Section shall be guilty of a Class 4 felony.

(2) A person who commits the offense of computer fraud as set forth in subsection (a)(2) of this Section shall be guilty of a Class 3 felony.

(3) A person who commits the offense of computer fraud as set forth in subsection (a)(3) of this Section shall:

(i) be guilty of a Class 4 felony if the value of the money, property or services is $1,000 or less; or

(ii) be guilty of a Class 3 felony if the value of the money, property or services is more than $1,000 but less than $50,000; or

(iii) be guilty of a Class 2 felony if the value of the money, property or services is $50,000 or more.

720 ILCS 5/16G-15 Identity theft

(a) A person commits the offense of identity theft when he or she knowingly:

(1) uses any personal identifying information or personal identification document of another person to fraudulently obtain credit, money, goods, services, or other property, or

(2) uses any personal identification information or personal identification document of another with intent to commit any felony theft or other felony violation of State law not set forth in paragraph (1) of this subsection (a), or

(3) obtains, records, possesses, sells, transfers, purchases, or manufactures any personal identification information or personal identification document of another with intent to commit or to aid or abet another in committing any felony theft or other felony violation of State law, or

(4) uses, obtains, records, possesses, sells, transfers, purchases, or manufactures any personal identification information or personal identification document of another knowing that such personal identification information or personal identification documents were stolen or produced without lawful authority, or

(5) uses, transfers, or possesses document-making implements to produce false identification or false documents with knowledge that they will be used by the person or another to commit any felony theft or other felony violation of State law.

(b) Knowledge shall be determined by an evaluation of all circumstances surrounding the use of the other person's identifying information or document.

(c) When a charge of identity theft of credit, money, goods, services, or other property exceeding a specified value is brought the value of the credit, money, goods, services, or other property is an element of the offense to be resolved by the trier of fact as either exceeding or not exceeding the specified value.

(d) Sentence.

(1) A person convicted of identity theft in violation of paragraph (1) of subsection (a) shall be sentenced as follows:

(A) Identity theft of credit, money, goods, services, or other property not exceeding $300 in value is a Class A misdemeanor. A person who has been previously convicted of identity theft of less than $300 who is convicted of a second or subsequent offense of identity theft of less than $300 is guilty of a Class 4 felony. A person who has been convicted of identity theft of less than $300 who has been previously convicted of any type of theft, robbery, armed robbery, burglary, residential burglary, possession of burglary tools, home invasion, home repair fraud, aggravated home repair fraud, or financial exploitation of an elderly or disabled person is guilty of a Class 4 felony. When a person has any such prior conviction, the information or indictment charging that person shall state the prior conviction so as to give notice of the State's intention to treat the charge as a felony. The fact of the prior conviction is not an element of the offense and may not be disclosed to the jury during trial unless otherwise permitted by issues properly raised during the trial.

(B) Identity theft of credit, money, goods, services, or other property exceeding $300 and not exceeding $2,000 in value is a Class 4 felony.

(C) Identity theft of credit, money, goods, services, or other property exceeding $2,000 and not exceeding $10,000 in value is a Class 3 felony.

(D) Identity theft of credit, money, goods, services, or other property exceeding $10,000 and not exceeding $100,000 in value is a Class 2 felony.

(E) Identity theft of credit, money, goods, services, or other property exceeding $100,000 in value is a Class 1 felony.

(2) A person convicted of any offense enumerated in paragraphs (2) through (5) of subsection (a) is guilty of a Class 4 felony.

(3) A person convicted of any offense enumerated in paragraphs (2) through (5) of subsection (a) a second or subsequent time is guilty of a Class 3 felony.

(4) A person who, within a 12 month period, is found in violation of any offense enumerated in paragraphs (2) through (5) of subsection (a) with respect to the identifiers of 3 or more separate individuals, at the same time or consecutively, is guilty of a Class 3 felony.

C. Web Activity

For information on how identity theft occurs, and how personal information can be kept safe, visit the Illinois Attorney General's web site on this topic:

►URL: http://www.ag.state.il.us/consumers/idtheft.html

III. Robbery

A. Comment

The Illinois statute defining robbery has remained essentially the same since the offense was codified. Terminology has been modified somewhat to more accurately reflect the elements which make up the crime. For example, "intimidation" was replaced by "threatening the imminent use of force" to clarify that element of the offense. The statute does not state an intent element. For a conviction, the prosecutor must establish that property was taken from the victim by force or threat of imminent force.

A person commits armed robbery when the elements for robbery are met and in addition, he or she is armed with a firearm or other dangerous weapon. Armed robbery is a Class X felony.

B. Statute

720 ILCS 5/18-1 Robbery

(a) A person commits robbery when he or she takes property, except a motor vehicle...from the person or presence of another by the use of force or by threatening the imminent use of force.

(b) Sentence. Robbery is a Class 2 felony. However, if the victim is 60 years of age or over or is a physically handicapped person, or if the robbery is committed in a school or place of worship, robbery is a Class 1 felony.

C. Case

The defendant appeals his conviction for attempted armed robbery alleging the State failed to prove him guilty beyond a reasonable doubt. Although a dangerous weapon was never displayed, he was found in possession of a "sharpened meat cleaver."

PEOPLE v. METCALFE
326 Ill.App.3d 1008, 261 Ill.Dec. 172, 762 N.E/.2d 1099 (1 Dist. 2001)

[Case citations omitted.]

Justice Sheila M. O'BRIEN delivered the opinion of the court:

BACKGROUND

At about 3:30 p.m. on January 8, 1998, Jerry Dudek was using an automatic teller machine (ATM) in one of the Citibank branches located in Chicago when the defendant, William Metcalfe, approached him and asked for money. Dudek said no. Defendant again asked for money. Dudek again declined. Defendant then brushed up against Dudek, stuck his left hand in his pocket, and said "I have got a gun. I want your money." Dudek begged defendant not to hurt him. Defendant responded by bumping Dudek and stating, "I want your f---ing money."

Dudek screamed for help while grabbing defendant's left arm, preventing him from taking Dudek's wallet from the ledge underneath the ATM. Defendant walked to a revolving door and attempted to exit the bank. Dudek put his foot against the door trapping defendant inside until he could be apprehended.

ANALYSIS

A person commits an attempt when, "with intent to commit a specific offense, he does any act which constitutes a substantial step toward the commission of that offense." A person commits armed robbery when he commits robbery (taking property from another by the use of force or by threatening the imminent use of force) while carrying on or about his person, or otherwise being armed with, a dangerous weapon. The officer testified at trial that defendant possessed a sharpened meat cleaver on his person. Any rational trier of fact could find that defendant took a substantial step toward robbing Mr. Dudek while carrying a dangerous weapon on his person. Accordingly, the State proved defendant guilty... beyond a reasonable doubt.

Defendant also argues that his conviction should be reversed because he never "physically manifested" the dangerous weapon (the meat cleaver) during the commission of the crime. We hold that defendant was not required to display or use his dangerous weapon to sustain his conviction for attempted armed robbery. Affirmed in part.

V. Arson

A. Comment

At common law, the crime of arson consisted of a willful and malicious burning of a dwelling house or outhouse within the curtilage (the enclosed space around the dwelling) of a dwelling house of another person. Over time, the Illinois arson statute was amended and separate statutes were adopted to include the burning of other types of structures, vehicles or personal property.

The present arson statute pertains to damage caused by fire or explosive to real property (land and attached permanent buildings) or personal property. Subsection (a) covers the property of another. For a conviction under this subsection, the State need not prove who owned the property, but at least show that it was owned by someone other than the defendant. Note that even if the defendant has a part ownership interest in the building or property, he cannot lawfully damage or destroy it. Subsection (b) covers one's own property that is damaged with the intent to defraud an insurer.

The corpus delicti for the crime of arson consists of two elements: (1) a burning; and (2) a fire of incendiary origin, meaning it was started by a person. For a successful prosecution, it is not necessary to show the defendant's motive. Nor is it necessary for the State to present their case through direct evidence since it is unlikely there will be anyone who saw the fire being set. The elements, therefore, may be established by circumstantial evidence. The requisite mental state is that the defendant committed the offense knowingly.

The crime of aggravated arson consists of the same elements of arson plus one of three aggravating factors listed in the statute. Aggravated arson is a Class X felony with a much higher maximum penalty due to the greater risk of injury to another person. A separate statute, residential arson, exists for burning the dwelling place of another.

B. Statutes

720 ILCS 5/20-1 Arson

A person commits arson when, by means of fire or explosive, he knowingly:

(a) Damages any real property, or any personal property having a value of $150 or more, of another without his consent; or

(b) With intent to defraud an insurer, damages any property or any personal property having a value of $150 or more.

Property "of another" means a building or other property, whether real or personal, in which a person other than the offender has an interest which the offender has no authority to defeat or impair, even though the offender may also have an interest in the building or property.

(c) Sentence. Arson is a Class 2 felony.

720 ILCS 5/20-1.1 Aggravated Arson

(a) A person commits aggravated arson when in the course of committing arson he knowingly damages, partially or totally, any building or structure, including any adjacent building or structure, including all or any part of a house trailer, watercraft, motor vehicle, or railroad car, and (1) he knows or reasonably should know that one or more persons are present therein or (2) any person suffers great bodily harm, or permanent disability or disfigurement as a result of the fire or explosion or (3) a fireman or policeman who is present at the scene acting in the line of duty, is injured as a result of the fire or explosion. For purposes of this Section, property "of another" means a building or other property, whether real or personal, in which a person other than the offender has an interest that the offender has no authority to defeat or impair, even though the offender may also have an interest in the building or property.

(b) Sentence. Aggravated arson is a Class X felony.

720 ILCS 5/20-1.2 Residential arson

(a) A person commits the offense of residential arson when, in the course of committing an arson, he or she knowingly damages, partially or totally, any building or structure that is the dwelling place of another.

(b) Sentence. Residential arson is a Class 1 felony.

C. Case

The defendant in the following case was convicted of arson based upon circumstantial evidence. Both the prosecution and the defense utilized the services of arson experts. The experts had very different opinions on how the fire in this case was started. The defendant did not testify at trial. It was up to the jury to decide whether the fire was intentionally set, and if so, whether the defendant was the one who started the fire.

PEOPLE v. SMITH

253 Ill.App.3d 443, 191 Ill.Dec. 648, 624 N.E.2d 836 (2 Dist. 1993)

[Case citations omitted.]

Justice MC CLAREN delivered the opinion of the court:

BACKGROUND

The defendant, Nancy Jean Smith, was convicted of one count of arson, following a jury trial in the circuit court of Ogle County. She was sentenced to three years in prison for the Class 2 felony. On appeal, defendant contends, *inter alia*, that the State did not prove its case beyond a reasonable doubt.

On March 17, 1990, fire broke out at the Kopy Kat Restaurant in Oregon, Illinois, some time shortly after the restaurant closed for the evening. The defendant, a waitress at the establishment, was charged on June 5, 1990, with one count of arson.

The defendant had been at the restaurant at closing time, 11 p.m. The defendant told investigators that she was the last person to leave the restaurant the night of the fire. The defendant was seen driving away from the restaurant shortly after 11:10 p.m. At 11:25 p.m. the chief of police of Oregon noticed "a white, foggish-type material" that turned out to be smoke near the Kopy Kat. The fire department was immediately summoned and arrived about five minutes later. The restaurant was well engulfed in flames at that time.

At trial, the State called an arson expert who testified that in his opinion the fire was incendiary (started by a human) and did not start accidentally. The State's expert believed that the fire started on the kitchen floor and that an accelerant (some type of fuel) was poured onto the floor. He further testified that only a deliberately set fire could have erupted so quickly from the time the last employees left the restaurant and the "fast, hot fire" was detected. No trace of accelerant was detected by laboratory tests.

ANALYSIS

It was uncontested that the Kopy Kat Restaurant was damaged by fire and that the restaurant was not the defendant's property. The only issues were whether the fire was accidentally or intentionally started and, if intentionally set, whether defendant was the person who started it. The case became a battle of experts.

The State's expert, detailed how he traced the source of the fire by looking for certain "pointers," such as burn and char patterns. He considered all possible causes and starting points for the fire and concluded that it started on the kitchen floor when an accelerant was poured onto it and ignited. Defendant's primary arson expert also undertook a thorough investigation of the fire scene and conducted tests. He was convinced the fire started accidentally and could not have started in the manner that the

State's expert believed. In short, the two experts, examining roughly the same information, arrived at opposite conclusions. The jury chose to believe the State's version. Viewing the evidence in the light most favorable to the State, any rational trier of fact could conclude that the fire was intentionally set.

The jury could also rationally conclude that defendant was the person who started the fire. The State's only evidence on this point was circumstantial: defendant was seen at the restaurant shortly before the fire began. However, the elements of the crime of arson may be shown by circumstantial evidence.

It was *un*controverted the defendant was the *last person* in the restaurant that night. She was there within 10 to 15 minutes of the time the fire was discovered. Although the defendant's mere presence at the restaurant shortly before the fire erupted does not *necessarily* imply that she set the blaze, such an inference is not so improbable or unsatisfactory as to constitute grounds for reversal. The close time frame in question dispels our concern that some interloper gained access and started the fire. Indeed, the defendant did not claim anyone else set the fire. The defendant's contention was that the fire was an accident. There was neither evidence nor argument of an interloper. For this court to reverse would require us to conjure up the possible existence of such an interloper. There was strong, credible evidence that the fire was intentionally set.

To be sure, this was a close case on the facts, and there was no direct physical evidence to link the defendant to the alleged crime. However, we note "the crime of arson is, by its very nature, secretive and usually incapable of direct proof." The circumstantial evidence in the present matter is similar to that which was adduced in *People v. Hanes* (1990), in which the Appellate Court, Third District, affirmed arson and burglary convictions. In *Hanes* the victim left her apartment at 8:30 p.m. and returned at 10 p.m. to find firemen outside of her apartment. After viewing the damage to her burned apartment, she walked outside to talk to police and saw the defendant, a former boyfriend with whom she had lived for six years before breaking off their relationship about a year before the fire, walking across the street. Police stopped defendant and recovered a clock radio from him that had been taken from the victim's apartment. As to whether the fire was intentionally started, the State in *Hanes* offered testimony by an arson expert who concluded after tracing burn patterns in the apartment that the fire started when a lamp either fell or was placed at the edge of the victim's bed and melted into the carpeting. No other sources of ignition were found.

The appellate court affirmed the arson conviction despite a showing that the jury specifically determined it did not believe the lamp started the blazed. The appellate court noted that the State was not required to prove the nature of the object used to set the fire, and that a rational trier of fact could have found the defendant guilty beyond a reasonable doubt. In the present case, though the facts were susceptible of more than one conclusion, the jury's finding was rational.

The conviction in the present matter must be affirmed.

D. Web Activity

Over the past decade, many communities have experienced an increasing number of unsolved arsons. In response, a number of governmental agencies have joined forces for training purposes and to share expertise in the investigation and prosecution of suspicious fires. One such example is the DuPage County Fire Investigation Task Force. Implemented on September 1, 1999, their goal is to assist local municipalities in processing and investigating significant fires of questionable origin. To access their web site for news and links, visit:

►URL: http://www.fireinvestigationtaskforce.com

IV. Burglary

A. Comment

At common law, a burglary consisted of the breaking and entering of a dwelling of another during the nighttime with the intent to commit a felony inside the dwelling. Over time, the Illinois statute has been amended so that the crime of burglary no longer requires a "breaking," or that it be a "dwelling house," or that the offense occur during the "nighttime." The intent element has been changed to include a theft as well as a felony.

Under the present statute, a burglary is committed when an individual makes an unlawful entry, or remains inside without authority, with the intent to commit a felony or a theft. The burglary statute not only applies to any part of a building, but also a housetrailer, watercraft, aircraft, motor vehicle, or railroad car. The requisite mental state is that the defendant made the unlawful entry "knowingly." The offense is complete upon the entry with the intent to commit a felony or a theft. The State need not prove that a felony or a theft actually occurred.

The offense of burglary is often proved by circumstantial evidence and the inferences which may be drawn from such evidence. Can a burglary occur at a Wal-Mart, for example, while the business is open to the public? Yes. Illinois case law makes clear that the authority to enter a business open to the public extends only to those who enter with a purpose consistent with the reason the building is open.

The burglary statute does not apply to a "dwelling" or "residence." The statute for residential burglary carries a higher maximum penalty. The elements are the same as for burglary with the exception that the place entered is where another person lives. For purposes of the residential burglary statute, the law defines what constitutes a "dwelling."

B. Statutes

720 ILCS 5/2-6 "Dwelling"

(a) Except as otherwise provided in subsection (b) of this Section, "dwelling" means a building or portion thereof, a tent, a vehicle, or other enclosed space which is used or intended for use as a human habitation, home or residence.

(b) For the purposes of Section 19-3 of this Code, "dwelling" means a house, apartment, mobile home, trailer, or other living quarters in which at the time of the alleged offense the owners or occupants actually reside or in their absence intend within a reasonable period of time to reside.

720 ILCS 5/19-1 Burglary

(a) A person commits burglary when without authority he knowingly enters or without authority remains within a building, housetrailer, watercraft, aircraft, motor vehicle as defined in the Illinois Vehicle Code [625 ILCS 5/1-100 et seq.], railroad car, or any part thereof, with intent to commit therein a felony or theft....

(b) Sentence. Burglary is a Class 2 felony. A burglary committed in a school or place of worship is a Class 1 felony.

720 ILCS 5/19-3 Residential Burglary

(a) A person commits residential burglary who knowingly and without authority enters or knowingly and without authority remains within the dwelling place of another, or any part thereof, with the intent to commit therein a felony or theft. This offense includes the offense of burglary as defined in Section 19-1.

(b) Sentence. Residential burglary is a Class 1 felony.

720 ILCS 5/19-4 Criminal trespass to a residence

(a)(1) A person commits the offense of criminal trespass to a residence when, without authority, he knowingly enters or remains within any residence, including a house trailer.

(2) A person commits the offense of criminal trespass to a residence when, without authority, he or she knowingly enters the residence of another and knows or has reason to know that one or more persons is present or he or she knowingly enters the residence of another and remains in the residence after he or she knows or has reason to know that one or more persons is present.

(3) For purposes of this Section, in the case of a multi-unit residential building or complex, "residence" shall only include the portion of the building or complex which is the actual dwelling place of any person and shall not include such places as common recreational areas or lobbies.

    (b)(1) Criminal trespass to a residence under paragraph (1) of subsection (a) is a Class A misdemeanor.

    (2) Criminal trespass to a residence under paragraph (2) of subsection (a) is a Class 4 felony.

C. Case.

    At issue in this case is whether the building the defendant entered fit the definition of a "dwelling" for purposes of the residential burglary statute. Note that the defendant was convicted of burglary, not residential burglary.

PEOPLE v. WILLARD
303 Ill.App.3d 231, 236 Ill.Dec. 679, 707 N.E.2d 1249 (2 Dist. 1999),
appeal denied, 184 Ill.2d 572, 239 Ill.Dec. 613, 714 N.E.2d 532 (1999)

[Case citations omitted.]

Justice MC LAREN delivered the opinion of the court:

BACKGROUND

    On or about June 17, 1995, a building owned by Ethan Olar, located in Dixon, was broken into and tools, compact disks, and a compact disk player were taken. Several days later defendant, Joseph Willard, was arrested while attempting to sell the stolen tools in Clinton, Iowa. Following a jury trial, defendant was found guilty of burglary and was sentenced to serve 7 years in the Department of Corrections. Defendant appeals his conviction.

    Defendant contends that he was not proved guilty of burglary beyond a reasonable doubt. According to defendant, the evidence at trial established that he entered a dwelling in violation of the residential burglary statute and, therefore, he could not have committed the offense of burglary. We disagree.

ANALYSIS

    For purposes of the residential burglary statute, a dwelling is defined as "a house, apartment, mobile home, trailer or other living quarters in which at the time of the alleged offense the owners or occupants actually reside or in their absence intend within a reasonable period of time to reside." Our supreme court has held that these offenses are mutually exclusive, in that residential burglary can be committed only in a dwelling, whereas burglary cannot be committed in a dwelling.

Ethan Olar was the owner of the building that defendant entered to take the tools, CDs, and CD player. Olar testified that the building had originally been a six-unit motel or hotel. Late in May 1995, he purchased the land on which the building and another structure stood. He planned to rehab the building into four residential units and a laundry room plus a residence for himself. Olar did not live in the building until approximately the middle of September 1995. As of June 16, 1995, no one lived in the building. On that date, much of the drywall inside had been taken down. One could see from one end of the building to the other on the inside. Olar described the building as "really not a place to live in yet" as of June 17, 1995.

Viewing the evidence in the light most favorable to the prosecution, we conclude that a rational jury could find defendant guilty of burglary beyond a reasonable doubt. The evidence at trial clearly showed that the building defendant entered was not a dwelling as defined in the statute. Therefore, burglary, not residential burglary, was proved beyond a reasonable doubt.

Defendant relies on three cases to show that Olar's building should be considered a dwelling; however all three cases are distinguishable. In the first case, the defendant's conviction of residential burglary was upheld where he entered and took items from the unoccupied first-floor and basement apartments of a building in which the owner lived on the second floor. At the time, the owner was rehabilitating the basement and first-floor apartments. At the time of trial, there was still no one living in the first-floor apartment, and there was no evidence regarding occupancy of the basement apartment. However, this case is distinguishable because in *that* case the owner was living in the building at the time of the illegal entry, although not in the units that the defendant entered, and was using the unoccupied space for storage. Here, Olar did not reside in the building at the time of the entry and never had.

Similarly, in the second case presented by defendant, the defendants were convicted of residential burglary of the unoccupied second story of a two-story building; the owners lived on the first story and were rehabilitating the second. The appellate court affirmed the convictions. This case is distinguishable because, once again, the illegal entry was made to a building that was occupied, the first and second stories were even connected by an inside staircase. Furthermore, there was evidence that the defendants had gone down to and taken items from the first floor, where the owners resided.

Finally, in the third case, the appellate court affirmed the defendant's conviction of residential burglary for taking items from a house that was not the actual residence of the owner. The prior tenants had moved out sometime before the entry, and the owner occasionally spent the night or the weekend at the house and stopped in every few days to pick up mail and check on the furnace and air conditioner. Once again, the building was inhabited, although this time not on an every-night basis. This case is clearly distinguishable based on the inhabitation of the building.

CONCLUSION

In the case before us, Olar's building was clearly not a dwelling. No one had lived in it, and no one currently lived in it. According to the evidence, no one could live in it at the time. Defendant's theory would make every partially built home, unoccupied and unoccupiable, a dwelling for purposes of residential burglary. This result is absurd. The statute requires that the occupants "actually reside *or in their absence* intent within a reasonable period of time to reside" in a dwelling at the time of the offense for residential burglary to apply. (Emphasis added.) "In their absence" implies that the building is habitable, but currently uninhabited, with a return to habitation planned shortly. An uninhabitable building does not fall within this definition. Furthermore, the entry into Olar's building did not implicate the concerns for privacy, sanctity of the home, and potential for serious harm that the residential burglary statute addresses. There is no home where no one can live, and no one's privacy can be violated where there is no habitation. With no one able to live in such a house, the probability of an intruder being confronted by the owner is nil. The dangers raised by residential burglary are not present to the same extent when a building is uninhabitable. We therefore conclude that defendant was proved guilty beyond a reasonable doubt of burglary and affirm his conviction.

D. Critical Thinking

▶ The defendant was convicted of Burglary, a Class 2 felony. Residential burglary is a Class 1 felony. On appeal, why did the defendant argue he was guilty of committing Residential burglary which carries a higher maximum penalty?

▶ What do you believe was the intent of the legislature in creating a separate offense for residential burglary?

▶ How does Criminal trespass to a residence [720 ILCS 5/19-4] compare to Residential burglary? Why is subsection (a) a misdemeanor and subsection (b) a felony?

E. Questions

Please choose the correct answer for the following questions.

1. Rex Rude came in through the bathroom window of his former girlfriend's apartment while she was asleep in her bedroom. Rex intended to take back the disco CD's he had given her. What, if any, crime did Rex commit?
a. burglary
b. residential burglary
c. criminal trespass to a residence
d. no crime, since the CD's had originally belonged to him.

2. Which of the following is an element of the crime of burglary?
a. entered recklessly
b. entered without authority
c. entered a dwelling
d. entered in the nighttime

3. While Max and Ima were in the process of getting a divorce, Max set their car ablaze in their driveway so Ima could not get possession of it as part of the property settlement. What, if any, crime did Max commit?
a. arson
b. aggravated arson
c. residential arson
d. no crime, since Max was part owner of the car

4. Zoe wanted to pawn her neighbor's DVD player. At noon on Tuesday Zoe entered her neighbor's house using the key that was kept under the doormat. Once inside, Zoe saw her neighbor had not gone to work that day. Zoe ran out of the house without taking anything. What, if any, crime did Zoe commit?
a. burglary
b. residential burglary
c. criminal trespass to a residence
d. no crime, since nothing was taken.

5. Just before midnight, Pat threw a Molotov cocktail through the office window of the Suds-O-Matic carwash in retaliation for having been fired earlier that day. The owner, who was working late that night, suffered third degree burns in the fire. With which crime will Pat most likely be charged?
a. arson
b. aggravated arson
c. residential arson
d. any or all of the above

CHAPTER TWELVE

Crimes Against Public Order and Morals

I. Disorderly Conduct

A. Comment

A violation of the disorderly conduct statute requires the offender knowingly engage in some activity in an unreasonable manner which would tend to disturb, alarm or provoke another. The Illinois statute has survived constitutional scrutiny. Courts have found the statute is not overbroad, nor is it unconstitutionally vague, even though the statute does not define the word "unreasonable."

Subsection (a)(1) may be violated in innumerable ways. Arguing with a police officer during the course of arrest, for example, has been found sufficient for conviction. The act constituting the offense need not be done in public view, nor does the language used have to be profane or vulgar in order to be unreasonable. The context of the parties' prior relationship may be considered in determining whether a violation has taken place, as evidenced by the case which appears in this section.

The subsections of the disorderly conduct statute other than (a)(1) define relatively specific acts which violate the law. Most involve some type of false report to an agency, but also included is what is commonly referred to as "window peeping." As you read through the statute, note the classifications for the different subsections.

B. Statute – Disorderly Conduct

720 ILCS 5/26-1 Elements of the Offense

(a) A person commits disorderly conduct when he knowingly:

(1) Does any act in such unreasonable manner as to alarm or disturb another and to provoke a breach of the peace; or

(2) Transmits or causes to be transmitted in any manner to the fire department of any city, town, village or fire protection district a false alarm of fire, knowing at the time of such transmission that there is no reasonable ground for believing that such fire exists; or

(3) Transmits or causes to be transmitted in any manner to another a false alarm to the effect that a bomb or other explosive of any nature or a container holding poison gas, a deadly biological or chemical contaminant, or radioactive substance is concealed in

such place that its explosion or release would endanger human life, knowing at the time of such transmission that there is no reasonable ground for believing that such bomb, explosive or a container holding poison gas, a deadly biological or chemical contaminant, or radioactive substance is concealed in such place; or

(4) Transmits or causes to be transmitted in any manner to any peach officer, public officer or public employee a report to the effect that an offense will be committed, is being committed, or has been committed, knowing at the time of such transmission that there is no reasonable ground for believing that such an offense will be committed, is being committed, or has been committed; or

(5) Enters upon the property of another and for a lewd or unlawful purpose deliberately looks into a dwelling on the property through any window or other opening in it; or

(6) While acting as a collection agency as defined in the "Collection Agency Act" or as an employee of such collection agency, and while attempting to collect an alleged debt, makes a telephone call to the alleged debtor which is designed to harass, annoy or intimidate the alleged debtor; or

(7) Transmits or causes to be transmitted a false report to the Department of Children and Family Services under Section 4 of the "Abused and Neglected Child Reporting Act;" or

(8) Transmits or causes to be transmitted a false report to the Department of Public Health under the Nursing Home Care Act; or

(9) Transmits or causes to be transmitted in any manner to the police department or fire department of any municipality or fire protection district, or any privately owned and operated ambulance service, a false request for an ambulance, emergency medical technician-ambulance or emergency medical technician-paramedic knowing at the time there is no reasonable ground for believing that such assistance is required; or

(10) Transmits or causes to be transmitted a false report under Article II of "An Act in relation to victims of violence and abuse," approved September 16, 1984, as amended; or

(11) Transmits or causes to be transmitted a false report to any public safety agency without the reasonable grounds necessary to believe that transmitting such a report is necessary for the safety and welfare of the public; or

(12) Calls the number "911" for the purpose of making or transmitting a false alarm or complaint and reporting information when, at the time the call or transmission is made, the person knows there is no reasonable ground for making the call or transmission and further knows that the call or transmission could result in the emergency response of any public safety agency.

(b) Sentence. A violation of subsection (a)(1) of this Section is a Class C misdemeanor. A violation of subsection (a)(5), (a)(7), (a)(11), or (a)(12) of this Section is a Class A misdemeanor. A violation of subsection (a)(8) or (a)(10) of this Section is a Class B misdemeanor. A violation of subsection (a)(2), (a)(4), or (a)(9) of this Section is a Class 4 felony. A violation of subsection (a)(3) of this Section is a Class 3 felony, for which a fine of not less than $3,000 and no more than $10,000 shall be assessed in addition to any other penalty imposed.

A violation of subsection (a)(6) of this Section is a Business Offense and shall be punished by a fine not to exceed $3,000. A second or subsequent violation of subsection (a)(7), (a)(11), or (a)(12) of this Section is a Class 4 felony. A third or subsequent violation of subsection (a)(5) of this Section is a Class 4 felony.

(c) In addition to any other sentence that may be imposed, a court shall order any person convicted of disorderly conduct to perform community service for not less than 30 and not more than 120 hours, if community service is available in the jurisdiction and is funded and approved by the county board of the county where the offense was committed. In addition, whenever any person is placed on supervision for an alleged offense under this Section, the supervision shall be conditioned upon the performance of the community service.

This subsection does not apply when the court imposes a sentence of incarceration.

C. Case

As the appellate court pointed out, this case concerned a long running feud between two commuters, who despite their mutual animosity, continued to travel the same route at the same time each morning on their way from their homes in Delevan to their jobs in Peoria. The defendant's actions one morning resulted in a conviction for disorderly conduct.

PEOPLE v. DAVIS
291 Ill.App.3d 552, 225 Ill.Dec. 597, 683 N.E.2d 1260 (3 Dist. 1997)

[Case citations omitted.]

Justice HOLDRIDGE delivered the opinion of the court:

BACKGROUND

Defendant, G. Wayne Davis, was charged by information with two counts of disorderly conduct, a Class C misdemeanor. Following a jury trial, defendant was found guilty of one count and acquitted on one count. By agreement of the parties, the matter proceeded immediately to sentencing and the trial court sentenced defendant to a $300 fine, ten days in the county jail...and one year probation....On appeal, defendant alleges, *inter alia*, he was not proven guilty beyond a reasonable doubt of disorderly conduct.

At trial, Beverly Larson testified that beginning in October 1995 defendant began to "harass" her on her commute to work each morning by doing such things as tailgating her car with his, positioning his car in front of hers while traveling down a two-lane road and then slowing down so that she could not pass, and following her to work, even to the point of running a red light to keep up with her. On one occasion, she returned to her car after work to find a note on her windshield, written by the defendant, which criticized her driving habits.

Larson testified that on the morning of January 19, 1996, she was traveling her usual route to work when she stopped to assist a stranded motorist whom she recognized as a friend. As she was getting in her car to continue on her way to work, she recognized defendant's car pass her traveling at about 60 m.p.h. within the flow of traffic. She waited until defendant had passed out of sight before she proceeded on her way. As she rounded a curve in the road a short distance from where she had stopped to help her friend, she discovered that defendant had "slowed way down" as if to wait for her to catch up with him.

Larson quickly caught up with defendant, although she slowed her car so as to maintain approximately two car lengths between their cars. Soon both cars approached a controlled intersection. According to Larson's testimony:

"A. When we got to Route 9, there was a lot of traffic and I got stopped behind him at the stop sign. There's a median to the left and a right turn lane that goes to the right. There were cars in the right turn lane that goes right. There were cars in the right turn lane and [defendant] was in front of me and my vehicle was behind his and there was a car coming up behind me. He got out of his vehicle and came back to my car."***

"A. I locked my doors real quick and rolled my windows up. He said, 'I'm going to be down where you work today,' and I shrugged my shoulders like this. He said 'I want you to stop tailgating me and stop harassing me.' I cracked my window and said 'Just get back in your car and go to work.' I said, 'I'm not tailgating you.' I said 'get back in your car and go to work.' He said some other things, and I said, 'Don't ever leave a note on my car again.' He said, 'Lady, I can go where ever I want and do whatever I want.'"

According to Larson, defendant walked back to his car and drove away after she picked up her car phone as if to place a call. Larson further testified that defendant spoke in a loud voice, but was not yelling, that he used no obscenities, and that she could not recall him using any hand gestures. She testified that she was very shaken by the encounter.

Defendant testified that Larson was tailgating him and following too close, so he stopped at the intersection, got out of his car and tried to reassure her he was not going to follow her that morning because he had to go very close to where she parked her car. He wanted to reassure her he was not following her and tried to tell her to stop tailgating and to leave him alone....

ANALYSIS

Defendant first maintains that his actions at the intersection on the morning of January 19, 1996, could neither alarm nor disturb another person, nor constitute a breach of the peace. We disagree....

First, the evidence...establishes that defendant knowingly committed an act in an unreasonable manner so as to alarm or disturb another, when he stopped his car in the roadway, thus blocking complainant's passage, and essentially trapping her in her car while he approached her. Complainant testified that she was alarmed and disturbed by defendant's action. Under the particular circumstances of the past history these two individuals had accumulated, any rational trier of fact could easily conclude that the complainant was alarmed or disturbed by defendant's actions.

Likewise, the evidence...establishes a breach of the peace. Although there is no evidence to suggest that defendant made overt threats against claimant or used profane or abusive language, it is well-settled that a breach of the peace can occur, even in the absence of such actions or language....

...[D]efendant's actions blocking complainant's way with his car, forcing her to remain behind him in her car, approaching her car on foot, and forcing her to listen to his comments about their disagreements and her driving habits, placed in the context of their previous relationship, was a form of harassment sufficient to constitute a breach of the peace.

We find, therefore, that defendant was proven guilty beyond a reasonable doubt of the offense of disorderly conduct.

D. Critical Thinking

►During defendant's testimony at trial, he admitted that he stopped his car at the intersection and went back to talk with the complainant. Considering the court's analysis, would the defendant have been found guilty regardless of what he said to the complainant?

►What could the parties have done to avoid this situation?

II. Street Gangs

A. Comment

The unlawful conduct of street gangs poses a special concern to those in the criminal justice system. The Illinois legislature has enacted statutes specifically designed to help combat gang activities. An example is found in 720 ILCS 5/12-6.1 which addresses gang membership. The statute states:

> A person who expressly or impliedly threatens to do bodily harm or does bodily harm to an individual or to that individual's family or uses any other criminally unlawful means to solicit or cause any person to join, or deter any person from leaving, any organization or association regardless of the nature of such organization or association, is guilty of a Class 2 felony.
> Any person of the age of 18 years or older who expressly or impliedly threatens to do bodily harm or does bodily harm to a person under 18 years of age or uses any other criminally unlawful means to solicit or cause any person under 18 years of age to join, or deter any person under 18 years of age from leaving, any organization or association regardless of the nature of such organization or association is guilty of a Class 1 felony.
> A person convicted of an offense under this Section shall not be eligible to receive a sentence of probation, conditional discharge, or periodic imprisonment.

In response to the increase throughout the State in the number of street gangs and related violent activities, the legislature enacted the Illinois Streetgang Terrorism Omnibus Prevention Act in 1987. The Act authorizes the State's Attorney to pursue a civil remedy against gang members in addition to any applicable criminal laws. The Act defines a "gang" in 740 ILCS 147/10, as follows:

> "Streetgang" or "gang" or "organized gang" or "criminal street gang" means any combination, confederation, alliance, network, conspiracy, understanding, or other similar conjoining, in law or in fact, of 3 or more persons with an established hierarchy that, through its membership or through the agency of any member engages in a course or pattern of criminal activity.

The legislative findings, as stated in 740 ILCS 147/5, address the situation as follows:

> (a) The General Assembly hereby finds and declares that it is the right of every person, regardless of race, color, creed, religion, national origin, sex, age or disability, to be secure and protected from fear, intimidation, and physical harm caused by the activities of violent groups and individuals. It is not the intent of this Act to interfere with the exercise of the constitutionally protected rights of freedom of expression and association. The General Assembly hereby recognizes the constitutional right of every citizen to harbor and express beliefs on any

lawful subject whatsoever, to lawfully associate with others who share similar beliefs, or petition lawfully constituted authority for a redress of perceived grievances, and to participate in the electoral process.

(b) The General Assembly finds, however, that urban, suburban, and rural communities, neighborhoods and schools throughout the state are being terrorized and plundered by streetgangs. The General Assembly finds that there are now several hundred streetgangs operating in Illinois, and that while their terrorism is most widespread in urban areas, streetgangs are spreading into suburban and rural areas of Illinois.

(c) The General Assembly further finds that streetgangs are often controlled by criminally sophisticated adults who take advantage of our youth by intimidating and coercing them into membership by employing them as drug couriers and runners, and by using them to commit brutal crimes against persons and property to further the financial benefit to and dominance of the streetgangs.

(d) These streetgangs' activities present a clear and present danger to public order and safety and are not constitutionally protected. No society is or should be required to endure such activities without redress. Accordingly, it is the intent of the General Assembly in enacting this Act to create a civil remedy against streetgangs and their members that focuses upon patterns of criminal gang activity and upon the organized nature of streetgangs, which together have been the chief source of their success.

Nowhere in the State are gangs a bigger problem than in the City of Chicago. According to Chicago Police Department statistics, there were 651 murders in the City during 2002 and 598 murders throughout 2003. Of the 598 murders in 2003, 43.2% involved gang activity (where a motive could be determined). More than one-quarter of the 2003 murders occurred within three Chicago Districts.

In 1992, the Chicago City Council passed the Gang Congregation Ordinance which prohibited "criminal street gang members" from "loitering" with one another or with others in any public place. Before the ordinance was lifted in 1995, police made over 42,000 arrests. In a 1999 decision in *City of Chicago v. Morales et al.*, the U.S. Supreme Court, agreeing with the decision of the Illinois Supreme Court, held the ordinance was unconstitutionally vague. The Court found the ordinance afforded too much discretion to police and too little notice to citizens who wished to use the public streets. It was suggested by one of the Justices however, that the ordinance could be rewritten in a way that would not violate the Due Process clause of the Fourteenth Amendment of the U.S. Constitution.

In 2000, the City Council passed a new anti-loitering ordinance allowing police to order suspicious crowds to disburse in certain high-crime areas. The rewritten ordinance appears below.

B. Chicago Municipal Code

8-4-015 Gang loitering.

(a) Whenever a police officer observes a member of a criminal street gang engaged in gang loitering with one or more other persons in any public place designated for the enforcement of this section under subsection (b), the police officer shall, subject to all applicable procedures promulgated by the superintendent of police: (i) inform all such persons that they are engaged in gang loitering within an area in which loitering by groups containing gang loitering within an area in which loitering by groups containing criminal street gang members is prohibited; (ii) order all such persons to disperse and remove themselves from within sight and hearing of the place at which the order was issued; and (iii) inform those persons that they will be subject to arrest if they fail to obey the order promptly or engage in further gang loitering within sight or hearing of the place at which the order was issued during the next three hours.

(b) The superintendent of police shall by written directive designate areas of the city in which the superintendent has determined that enforcement of this section is necessary because gang loitering has enabled criminal street gangs to establish control over identifiable areas, to intimidate others from entering those areas, or to conceal illegal activities. Prior to making a determination under this subsection, the superintendent shall consult as he or she deems appropriate with persons who are knowledgeable about the effects of gang activity in areas in which the ordinance may be enforced. Such persons may include, but need not be limited to, members of the department of police with special training or experience related to criminal street gangs; other personnel of that department with particular knowledge of gang activities in the proposed designated area; elected and appointed officials of the area; community-based organizations; and participants in the Chicago Alternative Policing Strategy who are familiar with the area. The superintendent shall develop and implement procedures for the periodic review and update of designations made under this subsection.

(c) The superintendent shall by written directive promulgate procedures to prevent the enforcement of this section against persons who are engaged in collective advocacy activities that are protected by the Constitutions of the United States or the State of Illinois.

(d) As used in this section:

(1) *Gang loitering* means remaining in any one place under circumstances that would warrant a reasonable person to believe that the purpose or effect of that behavior is to enable a criminal street gang to establish control over identifiable areas, to intimidate others from entering those areas, or to conceal illegal activities.

(2) *Criminal street gang* means any ongoing organization, association in fact or group of three or more persons, whether formal or informal, having as one of its substantial activities the commission of one or more of the criminal acts enumerated in paragraph (3), and who members individually or collectively engage in or have engaged in a pattern of criminal gang activity.

***

(e) Any person who fails to obey promptly an order issued under subsection (a), or who engages in further gang loitering within sight or hearing of the place at which such an order was issued during the three-hour period following the time the order was issued, is subject to a fine of not less than $100.00 and not more than $500.00 for each offense, or imprisonment for not more than six months for each offense, or both. A second or subsequent offense shall be punishable by a mandatory minimum sentence of not less than five days imprisonment.

In addition to or instead of the above penalties, any person who violates this section may be required to perform up to 120 hours of community service pursuant to Section 1-4-120 of this Code.

C. Web Activities

The Chicago Police Department developed the Information Collection for Automated Mapping (ICAM) system to provide residents of the City of Chicago with a tool to assist in problem-solving and combating crime and disorder in their neighborhoods. The data base contains maps, graphs, and tables with 90 days of reported crime information which can be accessed in blocks of up to 14 days. The data is refreshed daily, but the most recent information is back-dated 7 days. Search methods include: address, beat, intersecting streets, and schools. The information may be accessed at:

►URL: http://12.17.79.6/
►read and respond to disclaimer
►select a search method and enter information in other required fields

A summary of Index crimes for the City of Chicago may be accessed at:

►URL:
http://egov.cityofchicago.org/webportal/COCWebPortal/COC_EDITORIAL03YEHomicide.pdf

The Illinois State Police maintain information on the history, culture and activities of street gangs on a state-wide basis which may be accessed at:

►URL: http://www.isp.state.il.us/crime/streetgangs.htm

D. Statute

720 ILCS 5/12-6.1 Compelling organization membership of persons

A person who expressly or impliedly threatens to do bodily harm or does bodily harm to an individual or to that individual's family or uses any other criminally unlawful means to solicit or cause any person to join, or deter any person from leaving, any organization or association regardless of the nature of such organization or association, is guilty of a Class 2 felony.

Any person of the age of 18 years or older who expressly or impliedly threatens to do bodily harm or does bodily harm to a person under 18 years of age or uses any other criminally unlawful means to solicit or cause any person under 18 years of age to join, or deter any person under 18 years of age from leaving, any organization or association regardless of the nature of such organization or association is guilty of a Class 1 felony.

A person convicted of an offense under this Section shall not be eligible to receive a sentence of probation, conditional discharge, or periodic imprisonment.

III. Sex Crimes - Consenting Adults

A. Comment

The crime of prostitution is long standing in Illinois. There have been changes, however, over time. The Code now contains eleven prostitution-related offenses, seven of which pertain to adults, all of which are gender neutral. The prostitution statute prohibits the performance of, or offer to perform, any act of sexual penetration, or any touching or fondling of the sex organs of another, for anything of value, for the purpose of sexual gratification. It is also a crime to solicit a sex act from a prostitute, or to solicit on behalf of a prostitute. Illinois courts have recognized the State's interest in eliminating acts of prostitution due to the potential for causing crime and spreading disease. Law enforcement actively pursues offenders, as is evidenced by the case which appears in this section.

It may be surprising to learn that the Illinois Code section on sex offenses still includes the acts of adultery and fornication. Adultery, defined in 720 ILCS 5/11-7, prohibits a person from having sexual intercourse with another, not his (or her) spouse, if one of the two is married and the behavior is open and notorious. Fornication, defined in 720 ILCS 5/11-8 makes it unlawful for any person to have sexual intercourse with another, not his (or her) spouse, if the behavior is open and notorious. Adultery is a Class A misdemeanor while Fornication is a Class B misdemeanor. Unlike the crime of prostitution, these offenses are not actively prosecuted. Many states have repealed such statutes.

B. Statutes

720 ILCS 5/11-14 Prostitution

(a) Any person who performs, offers or agrees to perform any act of sexual penetration as defined in Section 12-12 of this Code for any money, property, token, object, or article or anything of value, or any touching or fondling of the sex organs of one person by another person, for any money, property, token, object, or article or anything of value, for the purpose of sexual arousal or gratification commits an act of prostitution.

(b) Sentence. Prostitution is a Class A misdemeanor. A person convicted of a second or subsequent violation of this Section, or of any combination of such number of convictions under this Section and [other listed] Sections... is guilty of a Class 4 felony....

(c) A person who violates this Section within 1,000 feet of real property comprising a school commits a Class 4 felony.

720 ILCS 5/11-14.1 Solicitation of a sexual act

(a) Any person who offers a person not his or her spouse any money, property, token, object, or article or anything of value to perform any act of sexual penetration as defined in Section 12-12 of this Code, or any touching or fondling of the sex organs of one person by another person for the purpose of sexual arousal or gratification, commits the offense of solicitation of a sexual act.

(b) Sentence. Solicitation of a sexual act is a Class B misdemeanor.

720 ILCS 5/11-15 Soliciting for a prostitute

(a) Any person who performs any of the following acts commits soliciting for a prostitute:

(1) Solicits another for the purpose of prostitution; or

(2) Arranges or offers to arrange a meeting of persons for the purpose of prostitution; or

(3) Directs another to a place knowing such direction is for the purpose of prostitution.

(b) Sentence. Soliciting for a prostitute is a Class A misdemeanor. A person convicted of a second or subsequent violation of this Section, or of any combination of such number of convictions under this Section and [other listed] Sections is guilty of a Class 4 felony....

(b-5) A person who violates this Section within 1,000 feet of real property comprising a school commits a Class 4 felony.

C. Case

The defendant, Patricia Hill, was convicted of soliciting for a prostitute, and co-defendant, Nancy Paris, was convicted of prostitution. Their cases were consolidated for appeal. The defendants contended the prostitution statute is unconstitutionally vague.

PEOPLE v. HILL
PEOPLE v. PARIS
333 Ill.App.3d 783, 267 Ill.Dec. 456, 776 N.E.2d 828 (2 Dist. 2002)

[Case citations omitted.]

Justice CALLUM delivered the opinion of the court:

BACKGROUND

Manis, a detective for the Lake County Sheriff's Department, testified at trial that on January 12, 2000, he performed an undercover investigation of a nightclub called Baby Dolls. Wearing a naval uniform, Manis entered the club, where various women were dancing in various stages of undress. Paris approached Manis and offered him a "fantasy dance." Manis accepted and paid $25 to a man who directed him to a chair.

After Manis was seated, Paris sat on his lap and began dancing, arousing him by rubbing her buttocks against his penis. The dance lasted through two songs. Manis was then approached by Hill, who explained that he could purchase a "sensual massage" from Paris. Manis paid $300 to Hill, who directed him to another booth. Paris sat next to Manis and put her legs across his. As music played, Paris unbuttoned Manis's shirt and rubbed his chest. She then used her right hand to rub his penis, arousing him. She resumed dancing on his lap, at one point "cupping" his penis and testicles in both hands. After about 30 minutes, Hill asked Manis whether he wanted to pay for additional time. Manis declined and left the club. Manis testified that his pants were never opened or removed. Paris never made "skin to skin" contact with his penis or testicles.

ANALYSIS

...It appears that neither the United States Supreme Court nor any federal or state court in Illinois has squarely addressed whether the constitution protects erotic dancing that involves physical contact with an observer....[The U.S. Supreme Court has] held that nude dancing <u>itself</u> 'is expressive conduct within the outer perimeters of the First Amendment.' It does not inevitably follow, however, that touching between a nude performer and a customer is protected expression. [The U.S. Supreme Court has also held that] intentional contact between a nude dancer and a bar patron is conduct beyond the expressive scope of the dancing itself. The conduct at that point has overwhelmed any expressive strains it may contain. That the physical contact occurs while in the course of protected activity does not bring it within the scope of the First Amendment."

...A mere erotic dance is constitutionally protected, but section 11-14(a) does not inhibit such conduct. Rather, an erotic dance may fall within the scope of the statute only when it involves specified physical contact between the dancer and an observer. When the dancer makes such contact, as Paris did with Manis, he or she is not engaged in a protected activity. Thus, section 11-14(a) does not inhibit the exercise of rights protected by the first amendment....

The defendants argue that section 11-14(a) is impermissibly vague for failing to define "sex organs." That assertion does not detain us long....Here, the defendants admit that, though the phrase "sex organs" is not defined, "one would presume that the phrase would encompass the human reproductive organs (i.e. penis and vagina)." Thus, because these prosecutions arose from Paris's alleged touching of Manis's penis, the defendants concede that the phrase "sex organs" is not vague as applied to their conduct. They cannot complain that the statute is vague as applied to the touching of something else, and we do not consider that argument.

Next, the defendants argue that section 11-14(a) is vague as applied to their conduct because it does not specify that it prohibits "any touching or fondling" through clothing. It appears that no court in Illinois has addressed this attack, but courts in other states have addressed similar claims.

We adopt the reasoning of [other courts and find that] Section 11-14(a) prohibits "any touching or fondling of the sex organs of one person by another person, for any money,***for the purpose of sexual arousal or gratification." The ordinary and popularly understood meaning of "any" is "one, no matter what one." Webster's Third New International Dictionary 97 (1993). Thus Section 11-14(a) unambiguously prohibits "any touching," no matter whether that touching is direct or indirect, on skin or through clothing. To read "any touching" to encompass only one kind of touching, rather than another, we would need to deviate from the statute's plain language and read into it a limitation that the legislature did not express. Such a reading would violate a basic rule of statutory construction.

Our conclusion is buttressed by the legislature's objective and the evil that it sought to remedy. Clearly, the legislature sought to prohibit any commercial transaction in which one person stimulates another person's sex organs for the purpose of sexual arousal. As Manis's testimony confirmed, a sex organ need not be exposed to be stimulated....The legislature sought to regulate the stimulation, not the dress code of the person stimulated.***

We conclude that, in prohibiting "any touching or fondling," Section 11-14(a) was specific enough to inform the defendants that touching through clothing was prohibited and to avoid the risk of arbitrary and discriminatory enforcement. Thus, on this basis the statute is not unconstitutional.

The judgments of the Circuit Court of Lake County are affirmed.

D. Critical Thinking

▶The offenses of Prostitution and Solicitation for a prostitute are both Class A misdemeanors for a first offense. Solicitation of a sexual act is a Class B misdemeanor. Why do you think the legislature made such a distinction?

▶Adultery is a Class A misdemeanor while Fornication is deemed a class B misdemeanor. How might the legislature have justified this difference in classification?

E. Questions

Please choose the correct answer for the following questions.

1. The offense of Disorderly Conduct requires:

a. the act be performed in public
b. the use of profane or vulgar language
c. the offender acted "knowingly"
d. a false report of some type

2. Which of the following is a true statement?

a. street gangs are a concern only in the inner-city
b. gang members have no right to harbor and express their beliefs
c. the State's Attorney may file a criminal and/or civil action against gang members
d. there are fewer than one hundred street gangs operating in Illinois

3. Violation of Chicago's gang loitering ordinance may result in:

a. a fine only
b. up to one year in jail
c. a fine and/or jail sentence of 6 months
d. a five year prison sentence

4. Law enforcement within Illinois actively prosecutes:

a. prostitution
b. adultery
c. fornication
d. none of the above

5. To be convicted of prostitution in Illinois, the defendant must:

a. be female
b. have made skin-to-skin contact
c. receive cash
d. touch the sex organs of another

CHAPTER THIRTEEN

Crimes Against the State

I. Terrorism

A. Comment

The Illinois statutes under Chapter 720, Article 29C, International Terrorism, were repealed effective December 5, 2002 by Public Act 92-854. The Act also addressed legislative findings, as stated in 720 ILCS 5/29D-5:

> The devastating consequences of the barbaric attacks on the World Trade Center and the Pentagon on September 11, 2001 underscore the compelling need for legislation that is specifically designed to combat the evils of terrorism. Terrorism is inconsistent with civilized society and cannot be tolerated.

> A comprehensive State law is urgently needed to complement federal laws in the fight against terrorism and to better protect all citizens against terrorist acts. Accordingly, the legislature finds that our laws must be strengthened to ensure that terrorists, as well as those who solicit or provide financial and other support to terrorists, are prosecuted and punished in State courts with appropriate severity. The legislature further finds that due to the grave nature and global reach of terrorism that a comprehensive law encompassing State criminal statutes and strong civil remedies is needed.

> An investigation may not be initiated or continued for activities protected by the First Amendment to the United States Constitution, including expressions of support or the provision of financial support for the nonviolent political, religious, philosophical, or ideological goals or beliefs of any person or group.

The Illinois statutes on terrorism are now contained in Article 29D. Selected statutes appear below. The mental state for terrorism is "knowingly" committing the act. The statute on hindering prosecution of terrorism does not require a mental state. The required element is the act of rendering criminal assistance to the person. The offenses of terrorism and hindering prosecution of terrorism are considered such serious offenses that both are Class X felonies. The death penalty may be sought for anyone convicted of terrorism should a death result from the act. As with a murder charge, a prosecution for offenses under Article 29D may be brought at any time.

B. Statutes

720 ILCS 5/29D-10 Definitions

As used in this Article, where not otherwise distinctly expressed or manifestly incompatible with the intent of this Article:

***

(l) "Terrorist act" or "act of terrorism" means: (1) any act that is intended to cause or create a risk and does cause or create a risk of death or great bodily harm to one or more persons; (2) any act that disables or destroys the usefulness or operation of any communications system; (3) any act or any series of 2 or more acts committed in furtherance of a single intention, scheme, or design that disables or destroys the usefulness or operation of a computer network, computers, computer programs, or data used by any industry, by any class of business, or by 5 or more businesses or by the federal government, State government, any unit of local government, a public utility, a manufacturer of pharmaceuticals, a national defense contractor, or a manufacturer of chemical or biological products used in or in connection with agricultural production; (4) any act that disables or causes substantial damage to or destruction of any structure or facility used in or used in connection with ground, air, or water transportation; the production or distribution of electricity, gas, oil, or other fuel; the treatment of sewage or the treatment or distribution of water; or controlling the flow of any body of water; (5) any act that causes substantial damage to or destruction of livestock or to crops or a series of 2 or more acts committed in furtherance of a single intention, scheme, or design which, in the aggregate, causes substantial damage to or destruction of livestock or crops; (6) any act that causes substantial damage to or destruction of any hospital or any building or facility used by the federal government, State government, any unit of local government or by a national defense contractor or by a public utility, a manufacturer of pharmaceuticals, a manufacturer of chemical or biological products used in or in connection with agricultural production or the storage of processing of agricultural products or the preparation of agricultural products for food or food products intended for resale or for feed for livestock; or (7) any act that causes substantial damage to any building containing 5 or more businesses of any type or to any building in which 10 or more people reside.

(m) "Terrorist" and "Terrorist organization" means any person who engages or is about to engage in a terrorist act with the intent to intimidate or coerce a significant portion of a civilian population.

***

(p) "Render criminal assistance" means to do any of the following with the intent to prevent, hinder, or delay the discovery or apprehension of, or the lodging of a criminal charge against, a person who he or she knows or believes has committed an offense under this Article or is being sought by law enforcement officials for the commission of an offense under this Article, or the intent to assist a person in profiting or benefiting from the commission of an offense under this Article:

(1) harbor or conceal the person;

(2) warn the person of impending discovery or apprehension;

(3) provide the person with money, transportation, a weapon, a disguise, false identification documents, or any other means of avoiding discovery or apprehension;

(4) prevent or obstruct, by means of force, intimidation, or deception, anyone from performing an act that might aid in the discovery or apprehension of the person or in the lodging of a criminal charge against the person;

(5) suppress, by any act of concealment, alteration, or destruction, any physical evidence that might aid in the discovery or apprehension of the person or in the lodging of a criminal charge against the person;

(6) aid the person to protect or expeditiously profit from an advantage derived from the crime; or

(7) provide expert services or expert assistance to the person. Providing expert services or expert assistance shall not be construed to apply to: (1) a licensed attorney who discusses with a client the legal consequences of a proposed course of conduct or advises a client of legal or constitutional rights and (2) a licensed medical doctor who provides emergency medical treatment to a person whom he or she believes has committed an offense under this Article if, as soon as reasonably practicable either before or after providing such treatment, he or she notifies a law enforcement agency.

720 ILCS 5/29D-30 Terrorism

(a) A person is guilty of terrorism when, with the intent to intimidate or coerce a significant portion of a civilian population:

(1) he or she knowingly commits a terrorist act as defined in Section 29D-10(l) of this Code within this State; or

(2) he or she, while outside this State, knowingly commits a terrorist act as defined in Section 29D-10(l) of this Code that takes effect within this State or produces substantial detrimental effects within this State.

(b) Sentence. Terrorism is a Class X felony. If no deaths are caused by the terrorist act, the sentence shall be a term of 20 years to natural life imprisonment; however, if the terrorist act caused the death of one or more persons, a mandatory term of natural life imprisonment shall be the sentence in the event the death penalty is not imposed.

720 ILCS 5/29D-35 Hindering prosecution of terrorism

(a) A person is guilty of hindering prosecution of terrorism when he or she renders criminal assistance to a person who has committed terrorism as defined in Section 29D-30 or caused a catastrophe...when he or she knows that the person to whom he or she rendered criminal assistance engaged in an act of terrorism or caused a catastrophe.

(b) Hindering prosecution of terrorism is a Class X felony, the sentence for which shall be a term of 20 years to natural life imprisonment if no death was caused by the act of terrorism committed by the person to whom the defendant rendered criminal assistance and a mandatory term of natural life imprisonment if death was caused by the act of terrorism committed by the person to whom the defendant rendered criminal assistance.

720 ILCS 5/29D-40 Restitution

In addition to any other penalty that may be imposed, a court shall sentence any person convicted of any violation of this Article to pay all expenses incurred by the federal government, State government, or any unit of local government in responding to any violation and cleaning up following any violation.

720 ILCS 5/29D-45 Limitations

A prosecution for any offense in this Article may be commenced at any time.

C. Critical Thinking

► In what ways has the legislature been mindful of an individual's or a group's First Amendment right to freedom of expression?

► The death penalty may be imposed for an individual convicted of an act of terrorism resulting in death. This law was enacted during the State's moratorium on executions. What message do you believe the legislature was trying to send by providing for such a sentence?

► What significance do you attribute to the fact that a criminal prosecution for any offense committed under Article 29D may be commenced at any time?

D. Web Activity

In May of 2000, the Illinois Terrorism Task Force (ITTF) was created by Executive Order for the purpose of identifying the strengths and weaknesses in the State's emergency response plans. The ITTF took steps to improve those plans and coordinate training at the local level even prior to the events of September 11, 2001. The ITTF, with representatives from all disciplines from throughout the State, now has the task of ensuring that the State is prepared to respond to a terrorist act.

To learn more about the ITTF, visit the Illinois Homeland Security web site at: http://www.illinois.gov/security/

Other sites of interest:

Illinois Emergency Management Agency (IEMA):
http://www.state.il.us/iema/

Illinois Department of Public Health: Bioterrorism Preparedness:
http://www.idph.state.il.us/Bioterrorism/bioterrorismfaqs:htm

II. Treason

A. Comment

Treason is most often thought of as an offense against the United States as defined in Article III of the U.S. Constitution. However, Illinois law provides for the criminal prosecution of such an offense against the State. For a conviction of treason, the Illinois statute requires the same proof as on the federal level: the testimony of two witnesses to the same overt act, unless the defendant confesses in open court. Like terrorism, the required mental state is that the defendant acted "knowingly." Also like terrorism, treason is a Class X felony for which the death penalty may be imposed.

The crime of Treason and other related offenses contained in Article 30 of Chapter 720 follow.

B. Statutes

720 ILCS 5/30-1 Treason

(a) A person owing allegiance to this State commits treason when he or she knowingly:
(1) Levies war against this State; or
(2) Adheres to the enemies of this State, giving them aid or comfort.
(b) No person may be convicted of treason except on the testimony of 2 witnesses to the same overt act, or on his confession in open court.
(c) Sentence. Treason is a Class X felony for which an offender may be sentenced to death....

720 ILCS 5/30-2 Misprison of treason

(a) A person owing allegiance to this State commits misprision of treason when he conceals or withholds his knowledge that another has committed treason against this State.
(b) Sentence. Misprison of treason is a Class 4 felony.

720 ILCS 5/30-3 Advocating overthrow of Government

A person who advocates, or with knowledge of its contents knowingly publishes, sells or distributes any document which advocates or with knowledge of its purpose, knowingly becomes a member of any organization which advocates the overthrow or reformation of the existing form of government of this State by violence or unlawful means commits a Class 3 felony.

C. Case

This case takes us back to a different time, a different war. The year was 1942. After war had been declared between the United States and the German Reich, Herbert Haupt left his home in Chicago, taking a circuitous route to Germany, where he received instructions from an officer of the German High Command so that he might join in destroying war industries and war facilities upon his return to the United States. Within days of his return to Chicago, Herbert was taken into custody as a saboteur. Shortly after his arrest, Herbert's father, Hans Haupt, was taken into custody and indicted for acts of treason for providing aid and comfort to his son and was convicted. The U.S. Supreme Court accepted the Petition filed by Hans Haupt and affirmed his conviction.

Not only is this case interesting from a historical perspective, but the Court's analysis is still applicable to the offense of treason.

HAUPT v. UNITED STATES
330 U.S. 631 (1947)

[Case citations omitted.]

Mr. Justice JACKSON delivered the opinion of the Court.

Petitioner, Hans Max Haupt was indicted for treason, convicted and sentenced to life imprisonment and to pay a fine of $10,000. From this judgment of the District Court for the Northern District of Illinois he appealed to the United States Circuit Court of Appeals for the Seventh Circuit, which by a divided court affirmed. A previous conviction of the same offense predicated on the same acts had been reversed.

Petitioner is the father of Herbert Haupt, one of the eight saboteurs convicted by a military tribunal. Sheltering his son, assisting him in getting a job, and in acquiring an automobile, all alleged to be with knowledge of the son's mission, involved defendant in the treason charge.

The defendant is a naturalized citizen, born in Germany. He came to this country in 1923 and lived in or near Chicago. In 1939 the son, Herbert, who had also been born in Germany, worked for the Simpson Optical Company in Chicago which manufactured lenses for instruments, including parts for the Norden bomb sight. In the spring of 1941 Herbert went to Mexico and, with the aid of the German Consul, from there to Japan and thence to Germany where he entered the employ of the German Government and was trained in sabotage work.

On the 17th of June 1942, Herbert returned to the United States by submarine. His mission was to act as a secret agent, spy and saboteur for the German Reich. He was instructed to proceed to Chicago, to procure an automobile for the use of himself and his confederates in their work of sabotage and espionage, to obtain reemployment with the Simpson Optical Company where he was to gather information, particularly as to the vital parts and bottlenecks of the plant, to be communicated to his coconspirators to guide their attack. He came with various other instructions, equipped with large sums of money, and went to Chicago.

After some six days there, Herbert was arrested on June 27, 1942, having been under surveillance by Government agents during his entire stay in Chicago. This petitioner was thereafter taken into custody and was arraigned on July 21, 1942. He later asked to talk to an F.B.I. agent, two of whom were summoned, and he appears to have volunteered considerable information and to have given more in answer to their questions. He blamed certain others for the predicament of his son and wanted to testify against them. For this purpose, he disclosed that he had been present when Herbert had told the complete story of his trip to Mexico, Japan, his return to the United States by submarine, and his bringing large sums of money with him. During his confinement in the Cook County jail he also talked with two fellow prisoners concerning his case and they testified as to damaging admissions made to them.

The indictment alleged twenty-nine overt acts of treason....Seventeen of the overt acts were withdrawn before submission and twelve were submitted to the jury. Generally stated, the overt acts submitted fall into three groups of charges: First, the charge that this defendant accompanied his son to assist him in obtaining employment in a plant engaged in manufacturing the Norden bomb sight; second, the charge of harboring and sheltering Herbert Haupt; and third, the charge of accompanying Herbert to an automobile sales agency, arranging, making payment for and purchasing an automobile for Herbert. Each of these was alleged to be in aid of Herbert's known purpose of sabotage.

The defendant argues here that the overt acts submitted do not constitute acts of treason, but that each is commonplace, insignificant and colorless, and not sufficient even if properly proved to support a conviction. We have held that the minimum function of the overt act in a treason prosecution is that it show action by the accused which really was aid and comfort to the enemy.

***

The most difficult issue in this case is whether the overt acts have been proved as the Constitution requires, and several grounds of attack on the conviction disappear if there has been compliance with the constitutional standard of proof. The Constitution requires that "No person shall be convicted of treason unless on the testimony of two witnesses to the same overt act...."

The act to be proved is harboring and sheltering in the house at No. 2234 North Fremont Street....It is sufficiently proved by direct testimony of two witnesses that the saboteur stayed in the house where the father lived and with the latter's knowledge. But it is said that this is not enough, that it fails because the two witnesses did not see him enter his parents' apartment therein. But the hospitality and harboring did not begin only at the apartment door. It began when he entered the building itself where he would have no business except as a guest or member of the family of one of the tenants. It is not necessary to show that he slept in the defendant's bed. Herbert was neither trespasser nor loiterer. He entered as the licensee of his father, and was under the privileges of the latter's tenancy even in parts of the building used in common with other tenants. His entrance to and sojourn in the building were made possible by the defendant, and the saboteur slept and stayed in some part of it with the father's knowledge and by his leave. We think the proof is sufficient to comply with the constitutional requirement that two witnesses testify to the overt acts in that group which charges harboring and sheltering of the saboteur.

The other group of submitted overt acts as to which it is claimed there is a deficiency of testimony relates to assistance which the defendant rendered to the saboteur in purchasing an automobile....[Witness testimony was corroborated] that the defendant came that night to the automobile salesroom, that he was accompanied by the saboteur, that a purchase of the automobile had been started and was pending. We think the court was justified in submitting this overt act and the jury was justified in finding it proved.

The Constitution requires testimony to the alleged overt act and is not satisfied by testimony to some separate act from which it can be inferred that the charged act took place. And while two witnesses must testify to the same act, it is not required that their testimony be identical. Most overt acts are not single, separable acts, but are combinations of acts or courses of conduct made up of several elements. It is not easy to set by metes and bounds the permissible latitude between the testimony of the two required witnesses....

One witness might hear a report, see a smoking gun in the hand of defendant and see the victim fall. Another might be deaf, but see the defendant raise and point the gun, and see a puff of smoke from it. The testimony of both would certainly be 'to the same overt act,' although to different aspects. And each would be to the overt act of shooting, although neither saw the movement of a bullet from the gun to the victim. It would still be a remote possibility that the gun contained only a blank cartridge and the victim fell of heart failure. But it is not required that testimony be so minute as to exclude every fantastic hypothesis that can be suggested.

We think two witnesses testified to these overt acts and petitioner cannot seriously contend that two did not testify to each of the overt acts comprising the group of charges on obtaining a job. Since this was the constitutional measure of evidence as to each overt act submitted to the jury we do not reach the question whether the conviction could stand on some sufficiently proven acts, if others failed in proof.

It is urged that the conviction cannot be sustained because there is no sufficient proof of adherence to the enemy, the acts of aid and comfort being natural acts of aid for defendant's own son. Certainly that relationship is a fact for the jury to weigh along with others, and they were correctly instructed that if they found that defendants' intention was not to injure the United States but merely to aid his son 'as an individual, as distinguished from assisting him in his purpose, if such existed, of aiding the German Reich, or of injuring the United States, the defendant must be found not guilty.' The defendant can complain of no error in such a submission. It was for the jury to weigh the evidence that the acts proceeded from parental solicitude against the evidence of adherence to the German cause. It is argued that Haupt merely had the misfortune to sire a traitor and all he did was to act as an indulgent father toward a disloyal son. In view however of the evidence of defendant's own statements that after the war he intended to return to Germany, that the United States was going to be defeated, that he would never permit his boy to join the American Army, that he would kill his son before he would send him to fight Germany, and others to the same effect, the jury apparently concluded that the son had the misfortune of being a chip off the old block—a tree inclined as the twig had been bent—metaphors which express the common sense observation that parents are as likely to influence the character of their children as are children to shape that of their parents. Such arguments are for the jury to decide.

***

184

It may be doubted whether the Constitutional reference to confession in open court has application to any admission of a fact other than a complete confession to guilt of the crime. The statements of defendant did not go so far. They were admissions of specific acts and knowledge as to which, insofar as they were overt acts charged, the required two witnesses also testified. There has been no attempt to convict here on such admissions alone, or to use the admissions to supply defects in the Constitutional measure of proof. If such an attempt were made we would be faced with a novel question. But here the admissions are merely corroborative of a legal basis laid by testimony and the Constitution does not preclude using out-of-court admissions or confessions in this way.

…The law of treason makes and properly makes conviction difficult but not impossible. His acts aided an enemy of the United States toward accomplishing his mission of sabotage. The mission was frustrated but defendant did his best to make it succeed. His overt acts were proved in compliance with the hard test of the Constitution, are hardly denied, and the proof leaves no reasonable doubt of the guilt.

The judgment is affirmed.

D. Questions

Please choose the correct answer for the following questions.

1. The mental state element of "knowingly" is required for the offense(s) of:

a. terrorism, but not reason
b. treason but not terrorism
c. both terrorism and treason
d. neither offense has a required mental state

2. The death penalty may be imposed:

a. for any act of treason
b. for any act of terrorism
c. for misprision of treason
d. for advocating overthrow of Government

3. Which of the following offenses is <u>not</u> a Class X felony?

a. terrorism
b. hindering prosecution of terrorism
c. treason
d. misprision of treason

4. For purposes of prosecution, the crime of treason against the State of Illinois is defined:

a. in the United States Constitution
b. in the Illinois Constitution
c. state statute
d. case law

5. The crime of treason may be proved by two witnesses:

a. who testify to the same act of the defendant
b. whose testimony is identical
c. both a and b
d. neither a nor b